THE ESSENTIAL
STUDENT COOKBOOK

Cas Clarke wrote her first book, *Grub on a Grant*, after taking a degree in Urban Studies at Sussex University. She now lives in Milton Keynes (and doesn't mind admitting it!) with her husband Andy and children James and Helena.

By Cas Clarke

The Essential Student Cookbook

Cas Clarke

headline

This edition first published in 2009 by HEADLINE BOOK PUBLISHING

1

Some recipes contained within this volume were previously published in *The Essential Student Cookbook* (first edition)

Cataloguing in Publication Data is available from the British Library

ISBN 978 0 7553 1872 8

Typeset by Avon DataSet Ltd, Bidford on Avon, Warwickshire

Printed and bound in Great Britain by Clays Ltd, St Ives plc

Headline's policy is to use papers that are natural, renewable and recyclable products and made from wood grown in sustainable forests. The logging and manufacturing processes are expected to conform to the environmental regulations of the country of origin.

HEADLINE BOOK PUBLISHING
An Hachette UK Company
338 Euston Road
London NW1 3BH

www.headline.co.uk
www.hachette.co.uk

Especially for James & Helena

Contents

Introduction

It's time to pack your bags and leave for university. Hurrah. Freedom! However, this also means having to cook for yourself, having to budget and trying to ensure that you have a basically healthy diet. This should all be part of the fun and it will be with just a little forward planning, whether you have any cookery skills or not. These recipes are quick and easy to make and will soon enhance your reputation as a cook. Some of them are from my previous books *More Grub on Less Grant* and *Vegetarian Grub on a Grant*. I have also added a few microwave recipes and some cocktails (alcoholic and non-alcoholic) and got rid of a few of the old favourites that seemed outdated and replaced them with new dishes that have proved very popular with friends and family. I hope this is the ultimate collection of all my recipes yet to be published. I had an added incentive as it's certainly the one that my eldest will be using at university, so I'd better not have left out any favourites or I'll be in trouble!

The original *Grub on a Grant* was written in 1984 and after many revised editions was followed up by *More Grub on Less Grant* in 1999. Ultimately these revisions found their way into this book. In those intervening years there had been a revolution in the way we shop and eat. Superstores are commonplace and stock a wealth of exotic produce that had not previously been available to us. Most people now are much more aware of what they eat and embrace more cosmopolitan flavours and ideas in cooking. Students have always been keen on big gutsy flavours – this is why dishes such as curry and chilli are enduringly popular – but there is a growing need as the tempo of life continues to increase for methods of cooking that produce meals quickly and easily, hence the popularity of stir-fried dishes, for example.

However, the biggest change of all has been the increasing emphasis on health and the realisation of how big a part our diet plays in keeping us fit. Fruit and vegetables have been made the focal point of our meals to be matched with rice, potatoes, noodles, pasta or bread to meet our energy needs along with just a little protein. The protein that we eat now is much more likely to be of vegetable origin; long gone are the days when it was thought that proteins from vegetable sources were second class. There were many recipes from *More Grub on Less Grant* that were suitable both for vegetarians and vegans. The reason for this is, of course, that vegetarian cooking tends to be less expensive than cooking with meat.

When all is said and done, the most important factor in *student* cookery is cost. That doesn't mean that a student can't eat well: it's just a matter of keeping away from costly items such as takeaways and ready-made meals. Students can also have particular problems (especially in halls of residence) with storage and facilities.

I am confident that this edition will show you how to overcome the problems of catering and that with it as a guide you, too, can become a competent cook who enjoys cooking both for yourself and for friends. I still firmly believe that nothing beats an evening spent with friends, wining and dining!

HANDY HINTS

It's important to have a healthy diet; by this I mean a diet that has a good amount of starchy foods, such as rice, pasta, potatoes and bread, complemented by fresh vegetables and fruit and some proteins, such as meats, beans, nuts or cheese. However, very few people actually stick to this diet. Most of us tend to eat more fats and sugars than we should. Alcohol, in particular, is very fattening and has no nutritional value.

If you find yourself putting on a few extra pounds, my advice is to look carefully at your eating habits before the problem escalates. Are you starting to snack on foodstuffs that contain high amounts of either fat or sugar? If your diet consists of a high proportion of chips, lots of pastry and cheese, crisps and chocolate bars washed down with copious amounts of booze, then you should not be surprised when you start to put on weight or break out in masses of spots! None of these items will hurt if consumed occasionally or in small quantities, but if you want to avoid ballooning you will have to restrict these goodies in your diet. The remedy is obvious: a week or two of a healthy balanced diet, with a ban on the offending goodies and an increase in your exercise regime – you do have an exercise regime, don't you? – should easily do the trick. Remember that bodies don't stay young and athletic naturally. If you then use a little discretion in the treats you allow yourself each week, you should avoid any further weight problems, which, in turn, lead eventually to health problems.

A BALANCED DIET

A balanced diet should consist of roughly 30 per cent starchy food, 30 per cent fruit and vegetables, 15 per cent lean protein, 15 per cent dairy products and 10 per cent fats.

Foods that can be eaten freely

FRUIT AND VEGETABLES

Most fruit and vegetables are low in fat and sugar content. (One exception is the avocado, which is high in fat – but it's 'good' fat.) Therefore, they should play a major part in your diet, preferably fresh, but even frozen or canned.

STARCHY FOODS

Examples of starchy foods are cereal, rice, pasta and potatoes. These are another very important group of foods, as they add bulk and ensure that you aren't still hungry at the end of a meal. However, it is very important not to add too much fat because starchy foods can absorb a lot of it.

Foods to be eaten in moderation

LEAN PROTEINS

These include lean meats, chicken, fish, beans, pulses and lentils. Although nuts are a good source of protein, they are very high in natural oils, so use them sparingly. Try to include two portions of protein in your meals each day.

DAIRY PRODUCTS

This group includes butter, milk, cheese and yogurt. These are important sources of calcium. As these can all be high in fat, you can either use them more sparingly or swap to the lower-fat varieties, such as skimmed milk and low-fat cheeses, spreads and yogurts.

Foods to be eaten only occasionally

FATS

Although we do need some fats in our diet, these are usually provided by the fat content of the other foods we eat. Therefore, we need to be very sparing in adding any extra. As well as cutting down the amount of fat we cook with or the dairy products in our diet, we must beware of such high-fat foods as ice cream, salad dressings, cakes, biscuits and pastries, chips and crisps, chocolate and many convenience foods.

ITEMS TO TAKE TO UNIVERSITY

ESSENTIAL

- [ ] knife
- [ ] tin opener
- [ ] wooden spoon
- [ ] cutlery and crockery
- [ ] tea towel
- [ ] small saucepan
- [ ] large saucepan with lid
- [ ] frying pan
- [ ] baking tray
- [ ] chopping board

REALLY USEFUL

- [ ] colander or sieve
- [ ] measuring spoons and jug
- [ ] mixing bowl
- [ ] whisk
- [ ] cheese grater
- [ ] garlic press
- [ ] vegetable peeler
- [ ] 1-person casserole dish
- [ ] 20cm flan tin – for pastry dishes and some sweet dishes
- [ ] corkscrew (some people would put this in the essential list – you know who you are!)

FOR COOKING WITH FRIENDS

- [ ] large casserole dish with lid
- [ ] lasagne dish or large roasting pan

Basic store cupboard

- [ ] ingredients to make your favourite hot and cold drinks
- [ ] favourite cereal
- [ ] yogurt or milk
- [ ] margarine or butter
- [ ] jam, peanut butter and/or Marmite
- [ ] eggs and/or cheese
- [ ] bread

THE IDEAL PARENTS WOULD ALSO SUPPLY

- [ ] dried borlotti beans or similar
- [ ] red lentils
- [ ] rice
- [ ] pasta
- [ ] couscous
- [ ] noodles
- [ ] cornflour
- [ ] tomato ketchup
- [ ] soy sauce
- [ ] olive oil
- [ ] korma paste and/or curry powder
- [ ] tomato purée
- [ ] stock cubes
- [ ] mixed herbs or oregano
- [ ] salt and pepper
- [ ] canned chick peas
- [ ] canned baked beans
- [ ] canned sweetcorn
- [ ] canned chopped tomatoes and/or passata (sieved tomatoes)

AND SOME FRESH VEGETABLES TO START YOU OFF

☐ potatoes   ☐ mushrooms

☐ onions   ☐ tomatoes

☐ mixed peppers   ☐ carrots

☐ garlic   ☐ courgettes

THE RECIPES

The chapters are roughly divided up into how long the dishes take to cook. Added to that, each recipe has a symbol or two attached to it so you can quickly see what type of meal it is:

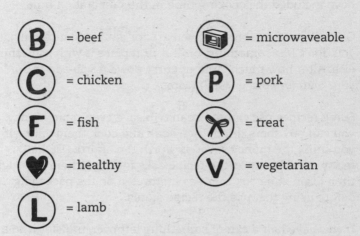

B = beef

C = chicken

F = fish

♥ = healthy

L = lamb

= microwaveable

P = pork

✗ = treat

V = vegetarian

The measures in all these recipes are approximate, so don't worry if the tin or jar you buy differs slightly from the one that I have used. The only time you need to be more careful is when you are cooking rice or baking. Different types of rice can absorb varying amounts of liquid, so be aware of this and keep an eye on these dishes. If you think the dish is drying out before it is cooked, turn the heat down and/or add a little more liquid.

Ovens vary enormously. If dishes are coming out overdone, turn the heat down by 10°C/50°F whenever you cook. Conversely, if dishes always take longer, increase the temperature by the same amount. If you are using a fan oven, you should reduce the temperature by 20°C/68°F and decrease the cooking times by 5 minutes for every 30 minutes.

Make sure if a recipe says 'gently simmer' that this is what you do; otherwise you could end up with a burnt pan and food. When grilling, make sure if you are cooking fatty meat that you beware of spitting fat or you could end up with a flash fire!

If you can leave the recipe to cook unattended for any length of time, I have put this under cooking time; if you cannot, I have included the cooking time in the preparation time.

Quantities of seasonings given are for your guidance only; if you don't like something, omit it or replace it with something else. Alter how much chilli or curry powder you add to suit your own (or your guests') tastes.

Some recipes use canned beans. To save even more money, you can buy them dried, then soak and cook them yourself (if you think the money saved is worth the effort). Use half as many dried beans as the recipe asks for. Soak them overnight, then drain and cook them as instructed on the packaging, before using them as the recipe states.

If you have half a can of something left over, transfer it to a container – a pudding bowl with a plate over it will do – and keep it in the fridge. If left in the tin, it may develop a metallic taste.

It's useful to have a plastic storage box with your name on it to keep items in the fridge. It's also useful to have some clingfilm to wrap half-used-up vegetables in – buy the local supermarket's economy version.

If you buy a supermarket's economy or own brand version of a food item, e.g. baked beans, whenever possible, you can make savings on many items. However, these items vary considerably in quality, so try them once before deciding to stock up. (You won't be saving money if you find them inedible.) Although I often specify cans of chopped tomatoes (being extremely lazy myself), it is cheaper if you buy the economy version of plum tomatoes and chop them yourself. Beware of buying a smaller tin that is actually more expensive than the bigger size! You will save money if you buy the bigger size even if you end up wasting half of it, but much better to store what's left in a plastic container in the fridge for a few days.

Many foodstuffs have to be kept in the fridge. With fewer preservatives in food, many items, once opened, have to be stored in the fridge and used up within a specified time. You ignore this at your peril, as the dangers of food poisoning are all too real and each year the number of reported cases goes up.

In this book, because by nature I am extremely lazy, I have used minced chilli and ginger in many recipes. Where minced chilli has been used, you can substitute ground chilli, dried chilli flakes or a fresh chilli, deseeded and finely chopped. Use whichever is most convenient for you – minced chilli wins hands down for me as the work has been done and the appearance is good when mixed into a dish. Its drawback is that it has to be kept in the fridge and used up within six weeks; if this is a problem for you, I would suggest buying either dried chillies, which can be crumbled into your cooking, or buying them fresh as needs dictate. Minced ginger has the same drawbacks as chilli but is even more convenient to use. However, you can substitute fresh ginger, peeled and grated, or very finely diced. A chunk about 3cm long is roughly the same amount as a rounded teaspoonful of minced ginger.

All teaspoon and tablespoon measurements are level;
1 teaspoon = 5ml and 1 tablespoon = 15ml.

A NOTE ON HYGIENE

I hope that somewhere along the way you've picked up that you should always wash your hands before starting to prepare and cook food. Common sense should ensure that anything used in food preparation should be clean. If there is one word of warning that must be worth repeating, it's the importance of keeping cooked and uncooked meat separate. I am always especially wary of chicken. Whenever you have touched raw meat, you must thoroughly wash your hands before continuing; otherwise, whatever else you go on to touch could become a breeding area for bacteria.

1 Snack Attacks
food to keep you on the move

As students are often in a hurry when it comes to preparing meals, it is important to have a range of snacks that can be quickly put together. In fact, the diet of many students consists of snacks, snacks and more snacks! If you are not to fall into the trap of living off takeaways and processed foods (expensive and not particularly healthy), this is certainly a good chapter to familiarise yourself with.

A big favourite with students is things on toast. However, sometimes you may have to share one small grill with a large number of other students (often all trying to cook at the same time), so it helps if you have a few other dishes that you can resort to if the queue for the grill looks too long.

Don't forget that if you can find time in the morning to prepare some sandwiches or filled rolls to take for your lunch, this is a good way to save money. However, this applies only if you then actually eat what you've prepared! If you end up going with friends to the canteen, you will have paid for lunch twice.

Just a quick word of warning on health: if you find yourself living mainly on snacks, it becomes even more important to include plenty of fruit in your diet. This is not difficult, as a piece of fruit is a ready-packaged snack. There is only so long the human body can take being stuffed with chips, crisps, pastry, biscuits and chocolate before it rebels with spots, obesity, etc. The choice is yours . . .

THE CHOICES:

EGGS

Fried Egg

Poached Egg

Scrambled Eggs

Scrambled Curried Eggs
with Chapattis

Full English

Egg, Tomato and Mushroom
Fry-up

Boiled Eggs and Marmite
Soldiers

American Pancakes

Huevos Rancheros

Cheese Omelette

Tomato and Spring Onion
Omelette

Cheese and Tomato Omelette

Eggy Bread

Frittata

BEANS

Baked Beans on Toast

Beans with Va Va Voom

Cheesy Beanz (microwave)

SANDWICHES/TOASTIES

Italian Fried Sandwich

Brie and Grape Sandwich

Peanut Butter and Banana
Sandwich

Stuffed Pitta Bread

Toasted Cheese

French Bread Pizza

Croque Monsieur

Melted Cheese and Tuna Bagel
(microwave)

Sardines on Toast

SOUPS AND SALADS

Leftovers Soup

Prawn and Leek Soup
(microwave)

Greek Salad

Avocado Salad

Hula Hoops Salad

DIPS

Crudités

Hummus

Tzatziki

Garlic Dip

Cheese Dip

Tomato and Garlic Dip

Sour Cream Dip

Guacamole

OTHER SNACKS

Avocado and Salsa Tortillas

Cheese and Chilli Nachos
(microwave)

Garlic Mushrooms
(microwave)

Glazed Nuts

Jacket Potato (microwave)

Chick Peas with Banana and
Mango

Special Fried Rice

Oriental Chicken (microwave)

Chunky Chicken and Mash
(microwave)

EGGS

Fried Egg

SERVES 1 • PREP 5 min

INGREDIENTS

oil for frying
1–2 eggs, depending on appetite

METHOD

1 Heat a frying pan and add enough oil to just cover the bottom of the pan.

2 Now crack your egg gently on the side of the pan and, opening up the shell, slowly slide the egg into the pan. Repeat with the second egg if you're using it.

3 Leave to cook gently for 1 minute then, using a spoon, gently scoop up some oil and spoon it over the yolk – this helps to ensure that the yolk and white are cooked at the same time.

4 When the yolk goes opaque and the egg white is set, the egg is ready – this is called 'sunny side up'.

5 Some people prefer their eggs cooked a little more. To do this, gently flip the egg over for a few seconds before serving – this is called 'over easy'.

TIP There are many uses for fried eggs – serve them with toast or even in a sandwich. They are great with beans or with oven- or micro-chips and some thick sliced ham.

Poached Egg

I love poached eggs but I rarely have them. I have found that to get a well-shaped poached egg you need really fresh eggs. So, if you have some, make the most of your good fortune and treat yourself. This is one of my favourite breakfasts served on a slice of sourdough toast or a toasted English muffin.

SERVES 1 • PREP 5 min

INGREDIENTS

1 *egg*

METHOD

1 Bring a pan of water to the boil. Make sure that there is a depth of at least 10cm of water in the pan.

2 Break your egg gently into a shallow cup or basin.

3 Now give the water a stir before gently slipping the egg into the middle of the pan.

4 Cook for 1 minute.

5 Cover with a lid, turn the heat off and leave for 2 minutes for a soft-set egg and 3 minutes if you like it a little more solid.

6 When cooked, remove the egg with a slotted spoon and drain briefly on kitchen paper before serving.

Scrambled Eggs

SERVES 1 • PREP 5 min

INGREDIENTS

2 eggs, beaten
1 tablespoon milk
salt and pepper
1 tablespoon soft butter or margarine

METHOD

1 Beat the eggs and milk together.

2 Season.

3 Melt the butter or margarine in a small saucepan and add the egg mixture.

4 Stir over a low heat for 1–2 minutes until the eggs are set to your taste. (Don't forget that they continue to cook a little after you take them off the heat.)

CHEESY SCRAMBLED EGGS

When you pour the egg and milk mixture into the pan, add 25g grated cheese.

Scrambled Curried Eggs with Chapattis

SERVES 1 • PREP 10 min

INGREDIENTS

knob of butter
1 teaspoon curry powder
3 eggs, beaten
2 tablespoons milk
salt and black pepper
2 chapattis

METHOD

1 Preheat the grill.

2 Melt the butter in a small saucepan and quickly stir-fry the curry powder for about 20 seconds.

3 Mix together the eggs and milk, season and add to the pan.

4 Stir-fry until the eggs are set to your taste (don't forget that they continue to cook a little after you take them off the heat).

5 Meanwhile, heat the chapattis under the grill.

6 Divide the mixture between the chapattis and roll them up.

TIP   Serve chapattis instead of rice with curries.

Full English

SERVES 1 • PREP 10 min

INGREDIENTS

1–2 tablespoons oil for frying
2–3 chipolata sausages,
  depending on appetite
2 slices bacon
1 tomato
several mushrooms
1 egg

METHOD

1 In a large frying pan, heat some oil and fry the sausages on a low heat.

2 Turn them so that they brown on all sides.

3 Add the bacon to the pan and again turn so that it cooks on both sides.

4 Cut the tomato in half and add it to the pan cut side down.

5 Depending on the size of the mushrooms, you can leave them whole or quarter or slice them. Add them to the pan.

6 Cook for 2 minutes.

7 Make a space in the middle of the pan and, if necessary, add a little more oil.

8 Break your egg into the middle of the pan and fry until the egg yolk is cooked. Serve.

Egg, Tomato and Mushroom Fry-up

SERVES 1 • PREP 10 min

INGREDIENTS

knob of butter
100g button mushrooms, cleaned
1 tomato, quartered lengthways
1 tablespoon oil
1 egg
salt and pepper

METHOD

1 Melt the butter in a frying pan and cook the mushrooms and tomato for 3–4 minutes.

2 Push them to one side of the pan, add the oil and, when it is hot, break the egg carefully into the pan.

3 Season with salt and pepper.

4 Baste the egg with the hot oil until it is cooked, then serve immediately.

Boiled Eggs and Marmite Soldiers

There are some who think that recipes for boiled eggs or for baked beans on toast are unnecessary. Perhaps they are unaware of the novice cooks who have tried to cook beans without first removing them from the tin or who have tried to fry onions whole and without first peeling them! It's difficult to decide just how much detail to go into but I like to think that if you have made it to uni in the first place, you must have some intelligence and common sense.

SERVES 1 • PREP 5 min

INGREDIENTS

2 slices bread
2 eggs (at room temperature – if taken straight
  from the fridge, they will crack when cooked)
butter or margarine
Marmite

METHOD

1 Toast the bread and boil some water in a saucepan.

2 Add the eggs carefully to the water and boil for 4 minutes.

3 Meanwhile, spread the toast with butter or margarine and Marmite.

4 Cut each slice of toast into 5 lengths and serve with the boiled eggs.

American Pancakes

SERVES 2 • PREP 10 min

INGREDIENTS

150g plain flour
2 heaped teaspoons baking powder
pinch of salt
284ml buttermilk or milk and water
2 eggs, beaten
butter for frying
maple or golden syrup to serve
bacon, cooked, to serve (optional)

METHOD

1 Mix all the dry ingredients together in a bowl.

2 Beat together the buttermilk (or milk and water) and eggs in another bowl.

3 Combine the wet and dry ingredients to make a batter.

4 Melt some butter in a frying pan and drop a tablespoon of the batter into the pan; it will start to form a pancake on touching the hot surface.

5 Drop more tablespoons of the mixture into the pan – you should be able to cook 3 or 4 at one time.

6 As soon as little air bubbles start to appear in the surface, turn the pancakes over and cook for about 30 seconds to a minute. If you take a look underneath, the pancakes should be browning. Remove them from the pan and add some more tablespoons of batter.

7 Keep the cooked pancakes warm in a low oven while you finish cooking the rest.

8 Serve with syrup poured over and bacon on the side, if you wish.

Huevos Rancheros

SERVES 1 • PREP 10 min

INGREDIENTS

230g can plum tomatoes, drained and flesh chopped,
  reserving 2 tablespoons of the juice
1 teaspoon finely chopped chilli
oil for frying
2 eggs

METHOD

1 In a small saucepan, heat the tomatoes with the reserved juice gently for 5 minutes, until reduced to a sauce.

2 Add chilli to taste.

3 Meanwhile, lightly cover the bottom of a frying pan with oil and heat.

4 Gently break in the eggs.

5 Baste with oil until the yolks become opaque.

6 Spoon the sauce on to a plate and arrange the eggs on top.

Cheese Omelette

SERVES 1 • PREP 5 min

INGREDIENTS

2–3 eggs, beaten
1 tablespoon milk or cold water
50g cheese, grated
salt and pepper
knob of butter

METHOD

1 Beat together the eggs and milk or water.

2 Add half the cheese and season.

3 Melt the butter in a small frying pan, and pour in the egg mixture.

4 Swirl the egg mixture over the bottom of the pan. Draw back the edges of the omelette from the sides of the pan so that any uncooked egg can run underneath.

5 When the egg has set, sprinkle the remaining cheese on top.

6 Gently fold the omelette and slide it on to your serving plate.

Tomato and Spring Onion Omelette

SERVES 1 • PREP 10 min

INGREDIENTS

2 teaspoons oil

salt and black pepper

2–3 eggs, beaten, depending on appetite

2 tomatoes, deseeded and flesh
  roughly chopped

2–3 spring onions, thinly sliced

1 tablespoon fresh chopped herbs
  (optional)

METHOD

1 Heat the oil in a frying pan.

2 Season the eggs and pour them into the pan.

3 Swirl the eggs over the bottom of the pan. Draw back
   the edges of the omelette from the sides of the pan so
   that any uncooked egg can run underneath.

4 Cook for 2–3 minutes until the omelette sets.

5 Add the tomato, spring onions and herbs.

6 Gently fold the omelette and slide it on to your serving
   plate.

TIP Fresh herbs suitable for this are basil, parsley, oregano or
tarragon.

Cheese and Tomato Omelette

SERVES 1 • PREP 10 min

INGREDIENTS

salt and black pepper
2 eggs, beaten
1 tablespoon oil
25g cheese, grated
1 tomato, chopped

METHOD

1 Season the eggs.

2 Heat the oil in a frying pan, then pour in the eggs.

3 Swirl the eggs over the bottom of the pan. Draw back the edges of the omelette from the sides of the pan so that any uncooked egg can run underneath.

4 The omelette should take only 2–3 minutes to set.

5 Add the cheese and tomato.

6 Gently fold the omelette and slide it on to your serving plate.

TIP You can vary the toppings using whatever you have in the fridge. Cooked mushrooms and broccoli make a good filling, or chopped ham (with or without grated cheese). To make an omelette for two people, double the ingredients and cut the omelette in half to serve.

Eggy Bread

SERVES 1 • PREP 10 min

INGREDIENTS

1 egg, beaten
1 tablespoon double cream (optional)
1 tablespoon full-fat milk
1 thick slice bread
knob of butter
1 tablespoon sugar
good pinch of cinnamon

METHOD

1 Mix together the egg, cream (if using) and milk. This is best done in a shallow bowl.

2 Dip one side of the bread in the mixture, turn it over and dip the other side.

3 Leave the bread in the bowl while you heat a small frying pan.

4 Melt the butter in the pan and then add the eggy bread. Pour any remaining liquid from the bowl over the bread in the pan.

5 Cook for 2 minutes on a gentle heat and then, when brown, turn the bread over and cook the other side for 2 minutes until brown.

6 Sprinkle with the sugar and cinnamon and serve.

TIP You can make a savoury version by omitting the sugar and cinnamon and serving it with tomato ketchup.

Frittata

SERVES 1 • PREP 10 min

INGREDIENTS

1 tablespoon olive oil
2–3 mushrooms, sliced
1 tomato, deseeded and flesh chopped
2–3 eggs, beaten, depending on appetite
salt and pepper

METHOD

1 Preheat the grill.

2 In a small frying pan, heat the oil.

3 Add the mushrooms and soften gently.

4 Add the tomato, stir once and then add the eggs. Season.

5 Make sure that the egg liquid is evenly distributed around the pan.

6 Cook for a few minutes until the eggs are setting.

7 Finish cooking the eggs under the grill. The frittata will look brown and puffy when cooked.

BEANS

Baked Beans on Toast

SERVES 1 • PREP 5 min

INGREDIENTS

2 slices bread
200–400g can baked beans,
  depending on appetite
butter or margarine

METHOD

1 Toast the bread while warming the beans in a small
   saucepan.

2 Spread the toast with butter or margarine and top with
   the beans.

TIP Grated cheese or chilli sauce can be added to vary this feast.

Beans with Va Va Voom

SERVES 1 • PREP 5 min

INGREDIENTS

½ x 430g can chilli beans
1 petit pain roll or 20cm French baguette
20g garlic butter, softened
25g cheese, grated (Emmental preferably)

METHOD

1 Preheat the grill.

2 In a small saucepan, heat the beans. Do not let them boil.

3 Split open the roll or baguette, spread with garlic butter and place on a heatproof tray.

4 Pile the beans on to the bread, sprinkle with the cheese and grill for 2–3 minutes until the cheese has melted and is bubbling.

Cheesy Beanz (microwave)

SERVES 1 • PREP 5 min

INGREDIENTS

200g can baked beans
25g Cheddar cheese, grated

METHOD

1 Place the beans in a microwaveable bowl, cover and cook for 1 minute.

2 Remove the cover and stir well.

3 Sprinkle with the cheese, re-cover and cook for 1 minute until the cheese starts to melt.

4 Stir the cheese into the beans before serving.

SANDWICHES/TOASTIES

I've given you some of my favourite recipes for sandwiches here, but the main advantage of sandwiches is their endless variety. You can ring the changes with the many different types of bread or rolls now available. Other options to consider are pitta bread, which is very good stuffed, or chappatis, in which you can roll up different mixtures.

Suggestions for fillings:

cheese with mayo and corn or chopped celery

cheese and pickle (vary the type of pickle)

cheese with cucumber or tomatoes

soft cream cheese with chopped celery and mayo

roast veg, pesto and mozzarella

hard-boiled egg with plain or curry-flavoured mayo

chilli or bean spread with lettuce and/or cucumber

peanut butter and jam (an American favourite)

corned beef and slices of pickled onions

cold sausage slices with barbeque sauce

roast chicken, mayo and spring onions

chicken and curried mayo

chicken with sweet chilli sauce

tuna, mayo and sweet pickle

Italian Fried Sandwich

SERVES 1 • PREP 10 min

INGREDIENTS

2 slices bread
50g mozzarella, grated
1 tomato, deseeded and flesh chopped
2 anchovies, drained and chopped
large knob of butter

METHOD

1 On one slice of bread, pile the cheese, tomato and anchovies.

2 Place the other slice of bread on top so that you have a sandwich.

3 Melt the butter in a frying pan and then carefully place the sandwich in the pan. Cook for about 3 minutes or until it is browning underneath.

4 Carefully turn the sandwich over and cook the other side for 3 minutes until brown, then serve.

Brie and Grape Sandwich

SERVES 1 • PREP 5 min

INGREDIENTS

2 slices bread
butter or margarine
25g Brie, sliced thinly
3–4 grapes, halved

METHOD

1 Spread the bread with butter or margarine.

2 Place the cheese on one slice of the bread, add the grapes and top with the other slice of bread.

Peanut Butter and Banana Sandwich

SERVES 1 • PREP 5 min

INGREDIENTS

2 slices bread
butter or margarine
2–3 teaspoons peanut butter
1 small banana, mashed roughly

METHOD

1 Spread one slice of bread with the butter or margarine. Follow with the peanut butter and then with the mashed banana.

2 Top with the remaining slice of bread.

TIP   Apparently this was a favourite of Elvis Presley – with a slight change. Although not recommended in large amounts, if you want to be like Elvis, make this sandwich and then fry it in hot butter until browned on both sides. Enough of these will certainly guarantee you'll grow more like him! (But may not improve your singing . . .)

Stuffed Pitta Bread

SERVES 1 • PREP 5 min

INGREDIENTS

1 pitta bread, split
50g feta cheese, sliced
1 tomato, sliced
1 teaspoon olive oil
1 teaspoon tomato or sun-dried tomato purée

METHOD

1 Stuff the pitta bread with the feta cheese and tomato.

2 Mix the oil and tomato purée and spoon it into the pitta bread.

Toasted Cheese

This is probably the most popular remedy for those late-night munchies.

SERVES 1 • PREP 10 min

INGREDIENTS

2 slices bread
50g cheese
2 teaspoons soft butter or margarine
1 teaspoon French mustard
dash of Worcestershire sauce

METHOD

1 Preheat the grill.

2 Toast the bread on one side.

3 Turn it over and toast the other side until it crisps but hasn't turned brown.

4 Mash the cheese, butter or margarine and mustard together and spread it over the toast. Add a dash of Worcestershire sauce.

5 Grill for about 2 minutes until the cheese is bubbling and starting to brown.

TOASTED CHEESE AND TOMATO SANDWICH

As above, but add 2 teaspoons tomato purée to the cheese mixture before toasting.

TOASTED CHEESE AND PICKLE SANDWICH

Follow the main recipe, but add 2 teaspoons of your favourite pickle to the cheese mixture before toasting.

French Bread Pizza

SERVES 1 • PREP 10 min

INGREDIENTS

2 tablespoons tomato purée
1 French baguette, split
sprinkling of oregano
50g cheese, grated
2 tomatoes, sliced
black pepper

METHOD

1 Preheat the grill.

2 Spread the tomato purée over the cut surfaces of the baguette.

3 Sprinkle with oregano and cheese.

4 Top with slices of tomato and season with black pepper.

5 Grill for about 2 minutes until the cheese has melted and is beginning to bubble.

Croque Monsieur

SERVES 1 • PREP 10 min

INGREDIENTS

2 thin white bread slices
1 teaspoon Dijon mustard
2 slices Gruyère cheese
25g thinly sliced ham
butter or margarine

METHOD

1 Preheat the grill.

2 Spread one slice of bread with the mustard.

3 Top with 1 slice of Gruyère, then the ham.

4 Top with the other Gruyère slice, then the other bread slice.

5 Spread the outside of the sandwich with butter or margarine and grill each side until brown.

6 Cut into two triangles and serve.

TIP Cheese and ham make a great filling for sandwiches or topping for omelettes or pizzas.

Melted Cheese and Tuna Bagel (microwave)

SERVES 1 • PREP 5 min

INGREDIENTS

½ small onion, sliced
small knob of butter
100g can tuna, drained
1 tablespoon mayonnaise
salt and pepper
1 bagel, halved
25g Cheddar cheese, grated

METHOD

1 Place the onion and butter in a microwaveable dish, cover and cook for 2 minutes.

2 Mix the tuna and mayonnaise together. Season. Add the cooked onion.

3 Put the bagel halves on a microwaveable plate, pile the tuna on top and sprinkle with cheese.

4 Place the plate in the microwave and cook for 1 minute until the cheese is melting.

Sardines on Toast

SERVES 2 • PREP 10 min

INGREDIENTS

2 slices wholemeal bread
150g can sardines in tomato sauce
dash of Worcestershire sauce
pepper
small knob of butter, softened

METHOD

1 Preheat the grill.

2 Toast each slice of bread on one side.

3 Mash together the sardines from the tin with a little of the sauce to form a rough paste, add a dash of Worcestershire sauce and season with pepper, then blend in the butter.

4 Use this mixture to spread over the untoasted sides of bread.

5 Grill for 2 minutes until the sardines are heated through.

SOUPS AND SALADS

Leftovers Soup

If you go home for the weekend, it is a good idea to scrounge some leftovers from the Sunday roast so you can make this soup very easily. It will feed one very hungry person or, with some bread, will make a good lunch for two.

SERVES 1–2 • PREP 10 min

INGREDIENTS

knob of butter
200g any cooked vegetables, diced
50–100g any roasted meat, diced
350ml chicken or vegetable stock
200g can baked beans
salt and pepper

METHOD

1 In a medium saucepan, melt the butter, add the vegetables and fry for 2 minutes.

2 Add the meat, stock and beans to the pan.

3 Season well and bring to the boil.

4 Cover, turn the heat down and simmer for 5 minutes.

Prawn and Leek Soup (microwave)

Sometimes you will find that supermarkets have prawns on offer. If so, this is a very good way of serving them.

SERVES 1 • PREP 10 min ı STANDING TIME

INGREDIENTS

large knob of butter
1 small leek, cleaned and sliced
medium potato (about 150g), peeled and finely diced
200ml fish stock (made with ½ fish stock cube)
125ml milk
75g raw prawns (king prawns if affordable,
   each cut into 2 pieces)
1 teaspoon cornflour
salt and pepper

METHOD

1 Put the butter and leek slices in a microwaveable bowl, cover and cook on high for 3 minutes until softened.

2 Add the potato and cook again for 3 minutes.

3 Add the fish stock, milk and prawns and cook for 1 minute until the prawns are cooked.

4 Mix the cornflour with 2 tablespoons of liquid from the bowl and then mix this back into the soup. Season. Microwave for 1 minute.

5 Let the soup stand for 2 minutes.

(continued over)

THAI PRAWN SOUP

Substitute coconut milk for the milk and add a dash of soy sauce and some dried chilli flakes. Don't use cornflour in this version and cook the prawns for 2 minutes.

Greek Salad

SERVES 2 • PREP 10 min

INGREDIENTS

several crunchy salad leaves
2 large tomatoes, sliced
½ cucumber, diced
several slices onion
2 tablespoons black olives
100g feta cheese, diced

FOR THE DRESSING

2 tablespoons olive oil
2 teaspoons wine vinegar
1 clove garlic, crushed
salt and pepper
squeeze of lemon

METHOD

1 Put all the salad ingredients into a bowl.

2 Mix the dressing ingredients and pour over the salad just before serving.

Avocado Salad

SERVES 1 • PREP 5 min

INGREDIENTS

1 avocado, stoned, peeled and sliced
1 little gem lettuce, shredded
4cm piece of cucumber, sliced
1 heaped tablespoon (25g) sunflower seeds

FOR THE DRESSING
2 tablespoons tomato ketchup
1 tablespoon soy sauce
1 teaspoon minced chilli

METHOD

1 Place the avocado, lettuce and cucumber in a serving bowl.

2 Mix together the tomato ketchup, soy sauce and chilli and use this as a dressing for the salad.

3 Sprinkle with the sunflower seeds.

TIP Use lettuce and cucumber as a filling for sandwiches – Marmite, lettuce and cucumber is a particularly good combination.

Hula Hoops Salad

This is a really crunchy salad that makes an ideal lunch dish –
but prepare it at the last minute or the Hula Hoops will go
soft.

SERVES 1 • PREP 5 min

INGREDIENTS

½ x 198g can sweetcorn, drained
2 celery sticks, sliced
2 tomatoes, sliced, or 6 cherry tomatoes
30g packet original Hula Hoops

FOR THE DRESSING
2 tablespoons cheese and chive spread
1 tablespoon natural yogurt

METHOD

1 Put all the salad ingredients in a serving bowl.

2 Beat together the dressing ingredients until smooth.

3 Dress the salad and serve immediately.

DIPS

Crudités

SERVES 2 • PREP 10 min

INGREDIENTS

2 carrots, cut into matchsticks
1 red pepper, cut into lengths
½ cucumber, cut in half and then into lengths
½ small cauliflower, divided into florets

METHOD

1 If you are not eating the vegetables immediately, store them in a plastic bag in the salad drawer of the fridge to keep them fresh.

2 When ready to eat, serve with your choice of dip.

Hummus

Tahini is not absolutely essential to this dish but it does add to its authenticity.

SERVES 2 • PREP 10 min

INGREDIENTS

400g can chick peas, drained, reserving the liquid
juice of 1 lemon
2 tablespoons tahini (optional)
2 cloves garlic, crushed
1 tablespoon olive oil

METHOD

1 Mash the chick peas to a purée.

2 Gradually add the lemon juice, tahini (if using), garlic, oil and 2 tablespoons of the liquid from the can of chick peas until you have a thick dip.

3 Chill before serving with toast or pitta bread.

TIP Leftovers will keep for a couple of days in the fridge and can be served with a jacket potato or thinned with a little milk and used as a sauce for pasta or rice.

Tzatziki

SERVES 2 • PREP 5 min

INGREDIENTS

200g Greek yogurt
¼ cucumber, finely chopped
1 clove garlic, crushed
2 teaspoons white wine vinegar
1 tablespoon fresh mint, chopped

METHOD

1 Mix together all the ingredients and serve as a dip or as
a sauce for rice dishes.

Garlic Dip

SERVES 2 • PREP 5 min

INGREDIENTS

2 tablespoons soft cream cheese
2 tablespoons single cream
2 tablespoons mayonnaise
2 cloves garlic, crushed

METHOD

1 Mix all the ingredients together thoroughly.

Cheese Dip

SERVES 2 • PREP 5 min

INGREDIENTS

125g soft cream cheese
1 tablespoon soft butter or margarine
1 tablespoon mayonnaise

METHOD

1 Blend together the cheese and butter or margarine, and then stir in the mayonnaise.

BLUE CHEESE DIP

To the above, add some crushed blue cheese, such as Danish blue.

CHEESE AND TOMATO DIP

To the main recipe, add 1 tablespoon tomato ketchup or purée.

Tomato and Garlic Dip

SERVES 2 • PREP 5 min

INGREDIENTS

2 tablespoons tomato purée
1 tablespoon olive oil
2 cloves garlic, crushed
salt and pepper
2 tablespoons hot water

METHOD

1 Mix all the ingredients together thoroughly with the water.

Sour Cream Dip

SERVES 2 • PREP 5 min

INGREDIENTS

150ml carton sour cream
2 tablespoons chopped chives
salt and pepper
1 clove garlic, crushed (optional)

METHOD

1 Combine all the ingredients, and pour them into a small serving bowl.

TIP Leftovers can be refrigerated for a couple of days. This dip is also very good served on a jacket potato.

Guacamole

In our house, this is a very popular dish. I often serve it with salsa and a sour cream dip and crudités and tortilla chips. My recipe often changes but this is the one we are using at the moment.

SERVES 2 • PREP 5 min

INGREDIENTS

1 large ripe avocado, peeled and stoned
1 tomato, deseeded and flesh chopped
sprinkling of chilli or cayenne pepper
squeeze of fresh lemon or lime juice

METHOD

1 Mash the avocado flesh to a smooth purée and then mix with the remaining ingredients. Serve with crudités or tortilla chips.

OTHER SNACKS

Avocado and Salsa Tortillas

SERVES 2 • PREP 5 min

INGREDIENTS

1 avocado

4 tortillas (warmed through before filling,
   if wished)

½ bunch of spring onions, chopped

50g cheese, grated

75ml sour cream or crème fraîche

2 tablespoons salsa

METHOD

1 Peel and remove the stone from the avocado, slice and divide among the tortillas.

2 Sprinkle each tortilla with spring onions and cheese.

3 Spoon the sour cream and salsa over the tortillas.

4 Wrap up each tortilla and serve.

TIP These can be served as a snack or with salad as a main course. If you have some leftover crème fraîche from another meal you could substitute this for the sour cream.

Cheese and Chilli Nachos (microwave)

SERVES 2 • PREP 5 min

INGREDIENTS

140g bag nachos
300g jar salsa – mild or spicy,
  depending on taste
150ml sour cream
80g Cheddar cheese, grated

METHOD

1 Put the nachos on a microwaveable plate, top with salsa and then sour cream.

2 Sprinkle the cheese over the dish.

3 Microwave for 2½ minutes so that the cheese is melting.

TIP Leftovers can be refrigerated and quickly reheated in the microwave.

Garlic Mushrooms (microwave)

SERVES 1 • PREP 5 min

INGREDIENTS

several mushrooms, quartered if large,
  leave whole if button
knob of butter
1 clove garlic, crushed
salt and pepper

METHOD

1 Put your mushrooms in a microwaveable bowl.

2 Dot the butter all over the mushrooms and then add the crushed garlic.

3 Season.

4 Cover and cook for 2 minutes or until the mushrooms are tender.

5 Serve on toast or as an accompaniment to eggs.

Glazed Nuts

MAKES ABOUT 300g • PREP 5 min • COOKING 5–10 min

INGREDIENTS

300g almonds or Brazil nuts,
  or a mixture of both
1 tablespoon butter, melted
1 tablespoon soft dark brown sugar,
  plus extra to taste
pinch of salt
pinch of mild chilli powder (optional)
1 tablespoon chopped rosemary leaves
large knob of butter

METHOD

1 Preheat the oven to 180°C/350°F/Gas 4.

2 Line a baking tray with foil.

3 In a medium bowl, mix the nuts with the melted butter, brown sugar, salt, chilli powder (if using) and rosemary. Put the mixture on the foil and spread it out.

4 Bake in the preheated oven for 5–10 minutes until warm and starting to brown – you can smell when the nuts are done. Do not overcook or they will burn.

5 Put the knob of butter into a bowl with the hot nuts and add some more sugar. Taste to see if you need any more sugar or salt. Best served warm.

TIP Keep these fresh for up to a week in a Tupperware or other sealed plastic container.

Jacket Potato (microwave)

SERVES 1 • PREP 10 min + STANDING TIME

INGREDIENTS

1 baking potato, cleaned

METHOD

1 Prick the potato all over with a fork.

2 Place a kitchen towel on a microwaveable plate and put the potato on that.

3 Cook for 4 minutes, then turn the potato over and cook for another 4–6 minutes until it is tender.

4 Remove the potato from the paper (or it will stick) and let it stand for 2 minutes.

TIP   Delicious with a bit of butter or grated Cheddar.

Chick Peas with Banana and Mango

This is a dish that is incredibly quick and easy to make and utterly delicious.

SERVES 2 • PREP 10 min

INGREDIENTS

430g can chick peas, drained
2 bananas, thickly sliced
½ x 230g jar spicy mango chutney
150g natural Greek-style yogurt

METHOD

1   Place all the ingredients in a saucepan and heat gently. Do not boil.

2   When heated through thoroughly, serve with cooked rice or pasta.

Special Fried Rice

SERVES 1 • PREP 10 min

INGREDIENTS

85g cubed pancetta
2–3 mushrooms, sliced
several cooked peas or some diced green pepper
1 tablespoon oil
50g cooked rice
100g canned sweetcorn, drained
1 egg, beaten
dash of soy sauce

METHOD

1 In a frying pan, cook the pancetta, mushrooms and green vegetables in the oil until the bacon is starting to crisp and brown.

2 Add the rice and sweetcorn and stir well.

3 Make a little space in the bottom of the pan and add a little of the egg to this. As it cooks, stir it into the rice.

4 Repeat until all the egg is cooked.

5 Season with soy sauce and serve.

TIP Put the rice in a sieve and run cold water through it before cooking. This helps to prevent it from sticking together.
Fried rice is always better made with cold cooked rice. Once cooked, cool completely, cover and refrigerate until ready to use. Always recook rice thoroughly before eating.

Oriental Chicken (microwave)

SERVES 1 • PREP 10 min

INGREDIENTS

1 chicken breast fillet, skinless, sliced thinly
1 tablespoon soy sauce
1 teaspoon honey
1 tablespoon tomato ketchup
1 teaspoon cornflour
1 tablespoon water

METHOD

1 Place all the ingredients except the cornflour and water in a microwaveable dish, and stir well.

2 Cover and cook for 4 minutes or until the chicken is cooked through.

3 Mix cornflour with the water and stir this into the sauce. Cover and cook for 1 minute.

4 Serve with microwaveable rice or noodles. This also goes well with canned sweetcorn.

Chunky Chicken and Mash (microwave)

SERVES 1 • PREP 5 min + STANDING TIME

INGREDIENTS

80g frozen broad beans or peas
206g can chunky chicken in white sauce
1 serving (30g) dried mash

METHOD

1 Place the vegetables in a microwaveable dish.

2 Cover and cook for 1 minute.

3 Add the chicken with its sauce and stir.

4 Cook for 2 minutes.

5 Make up the mash as directed on the packet.

6 Stir the chicken mixture and then top with the mash.

7 Cook for 30 seconds.

8 Let it stand for 2 minutes.

TIP This is a recipe that can be adapted in many ways: you can use chunky steak or mince in gravy instead of the chunky chicken; you can vary the vegetables, using cans of beans, carrots, sweetcorn, etc. You can get frozen mash, which you can quickly defrost in the microwave and then use to top your dish. You can use broken-up tacos or crisps sprinkled with a little cheese as toppings. I'm sure you'll come up with your own favourite recipe.

---

2 The Hairy Hall Experience
cooking for 1 or 2 in under 20 minutes

What makes cooking conditions so different in halls of residence? First, facilities are generally not up to much and many people have to share them, so you want to get in and out of the kitchen fast. Fridge space is also at a premium and items can go missing! I have assumed, too, that little money is available for a stock cupboard so such items do not feature heavily.

It's a well-known fact that many people, faced with cooking for one, just don't bother. But . . . it is a good way of saving money and it's better for your diet than continually living off processed food. (Look at the ingredients next time you buy a ready-made meal – do you really want all those additives?) There are many meals for one or two that can be cooked in minutes and are really very easy to prepare. At the beginning of term being busy in the kitchen is a great way of meeting people and making new friends. (Many years later, two of my best friends are people I shared a kitchen with that first year.) So even if you haven't had a great deal to do with the kitchen up until now, this is the time to enjoy its pleasures!

I know that it can be difficult to buy really fresh vegetables on campus and here I have kept mainly to the veggie staples of the student diet, i.e. onions, peppers, tomatoes, mushrooms and carrots. However, even with all these problems, it can still be possible to eat well when in hall. In many recipes in this book, I have used items such as minced chilli and ginger because of the convenience factor. Since they have to be kept in the fridge and you may have problems with marauding bands of thieves or 'borrowers', while in hall you may be better off substituting dried chillies and fresh ginger, as these keep well and can often be bought in small quantities in supermarkets and sometimes even from campus shops.

These recipes are quick and easy to make and very cosmopolitan in flavour, so they are ideal for students who are just beginning to cook.

THE CHOICES:

SOUPS AND SALADS

Mexican Bean Soup

Red Lentil and Apple Soup

Hasta Arriba Salad

Italian Tuna and Bean Salad

POTATOES

Cheese and Marmite Jacket (microwave)

Jacket Potato Filled with Chilli Beans (microwave)

Jacket Potatoes Filled with Garlic Cheese and Mushrooms (microwave)

Tuna-stuffed Jacket Potatoes (microwave)

VEGGIE DISHES

Student Standby

Veggie Varsity Pie

Mushroom Stroganoff

Creamy Courgettes and Walnuts

Pipérade

Veggies in Cheese Sauce

Cheesy Rice (microwave)

Hot 'n' Spicy Vegetable Couscous

Cheese and Tomato Vegetables

Rice, Potatoes and Onions

Chilli and Garlic Beans

Beer Fondue

Cheese Fondue

PASTA DISHES

Sun-dried Tomato Risotto

Quick Fried Cheese 'n' Tomato Pizza

Dolcelatte-dressed Spaghetti and Leeks

Pasta and Mushrooms with Hummus Sauce

Avocado and Banana with Pasta

Tomato Provençale and Spaghetti

Mushroom and Hazelnut Sauce (for Pasta)

Pasta with Creamy Salmon Sauce

Tuna and Green Pepper Sauce and Pasta

Spaghetti Carbonara

Spaghetti Tricolor

Spaghetti Putanesca

Pasta Alfredo

Pasta with Walnuts

Creamed Leek and Courgette Sauce (for Pasta)

Broccoli Sauce (for Pasta)

Spaghetti Tunagnese

Pasta Frittata

Spaghetti with Anchovies and Garlic Crumbs

Pasta with Tomato and Garlic

Pasta with Cheese 'n' Garlic Sauce

STIR-FRIES AND CURRIES

Thai Prawns

Stir-fried Beef in Oyster Sauce

Chilli Vegetables and Noodles

Thai Lamb

Quick-fix Chicken Noodles

Chinese Rice with Omelette

Sweet 'n' Sour Chicken and Rice Dish (microwave)

Chinese Vegetables and Noodles (microwave)

Thai Noodles

Sweet 'n' Sour Vegetables

Chicken Chow Mein

Vegetable Chow Mein

Stir-fried Broccoli and Cashews

Prawns in Lime Ginger Butter

Egg and Lentil Curry

Fish with Coconut Curry Relish (microwave)

Spicy Rice

MEAT DISHES

Barbecued Pork Chop

Honey-glazed Lamb Steak

Lamb in Mustard Cream
Sauce

Microwave Chilli

Mince-stuffed Peppers
(microwave)

SOUPS AND SALADS

Mexican Bean Soup

This is a really easy soup to make and is a great supper dish. Smaller portions would make a delicious starter for a Mexican meal.

SERVES 1 • PREP 20 min

INGREDIENTS

1 tablespoon oil
1 small onion, chopped
1 small green pepper, diced
215g can beans in spicy/chilli sauce
200g can chopped tomatoes
tortilla chips to serve
grated cheese to serve

METHOD

1 Heat the oil in a small saucepan and fry the onion and pepper for 5 minutes until they are soft and starting to brown.

2 Add the beans and tomatoes and stir well.

3 Simmer gently for 10 minutes.

4 Serve topped with tortilla chips and grated cheese.

Red Lentil and Apple Soup

SERVES 2 • PREP 10 min • COOKING 20 min

INGREDIENTS

large knob of butter
1 onion, chopped
2 small/medium carrots
  (about 100g), finely chopped
100g dried red lentils
1 small eating apple, peeled, cored and diced
750ml vegetable stock (made with 1 stock cube)
small pinch of mixed herbs or oregano
salt and pepper

METHOD

1 In a medium saucepan, melt the butter and gently fry
   the onion and carrots until they start to soften and
   brown.

2 Add the lentils and apple and stir-fry for 1–2 minutes.

3 Add the stock and herbs, bring to the boil, cover and
   cook gently for 10 minutes.

4 Season well, stir and serve.

Hasta Arriba Salad

SERVES 2 • PREP 10 min

INGREDIENTS

1 tablespoon oil
250g minced beef
2 cloves garlic, crushed
1 tablespoon tomato purée
50ml water
1–2 teaspoons minced chilli
200g can red kidney beans,
   drained and rinsed
salt and black pepper

FOR THE SALAD

lettuce leaves, shredded
½ cucumber, halved lengthways
   and sliced
2 tomatoes, cut into wedges
40g packet tortilla chips

METHOD

1 Heat the oil in a pan and fry the beef for 5 minutes until the meat has browned.

2 Add the garlic and quickly stir-fry for 20–30 seconds. Don't let it burn.

3 Stir in the tomato purée, water, chilli and kidney beans, season and stir-fry for a few minutes to heat through.

4 Meanwhile, mix together the salad ingredients and divide between 2 bowls.

5 Pile the hot mince on to the salad and serve.

TIP This salad is even better served with some grated cheese and sour cream.

Italian Tuna and Bean Salad

SERVES 2 • PREP 10 min

INGREDIENTS

4 tablespoons (60ml) olive oil
1 onion, sliced into rings
½ tablespoon white wine vinegar
1 clove garlic, crushed
400g can cannellini beans, drained
185g can tuna, drained and flaked
salt and black pepper

METHOD

1 Heat 1 tablespoon of the oil in a pan and fry the onion until it is soft and starting to brown.

2 Put the rest of the oil, the vinegar and the garlic in a clean screw-top jar and shake well.

3 In a bowl, gently mix together the onions, beans and tuna.

4 Drizzle with the dressing, season well and serve.

POTATOES

Cheese and Marmite Jacket (microwave)

SERVES 1 • PREP 10 min

INGREDIENTS

1 baking potato, cleaned
knob of butter or margarine
large dab of Marmite
  (you know your own taste!)
25g Cheddar cheese, grated

METHOD

1 Prick the potato all over with a fork.

2 Place a kitchen towel on a microwaveable plate and put the potato on that.

3 Cook for 4 minutes, then turn the potato over and cook for another 4–6 minutes until it is tender.

4 Remove from the microwave.

5 Using a clean tea towel to protect your hands, cut the potato in half lengthways.

(continued over)

6 Scoop out the flesh and mash with the butter or margarine and Marmite. Mix in the cheese.

7 Pile the mash back into the skins and place on a microwaveable plate.

8 Cook for 1 minute.

Jacket Potato Filled with Chilli Beans (microwave)

SERVES 1 • PREP 5 min • COOKING 10 min + STANDING TIME

INGREDIENTS

1 *large potato*

FOR THE FILLING
215g *can chilli beans*

METHOD

1 Prick the potato all over with a fork.

2 Place a kitchen towel on a microwaveable plate and put the potato on that.

3 Cook for 4 minutes, then turn the potato over and cook for another 4–6 minutes until it is tender.

4 Remove the potato from the paper (or it will stick) and let it stand for 2 minutes.

5 Meanwhile, place the opened beans in a microwaveable dish and heat through.

6 Cut a large cross in the top of the potato and squeeze gently to open it out, then top with the chilli beans.

TIP Jacket potatoes can also be served with baked, barbecued or curried beans.

Jacket Potatoes Filled with Garlic Cheese and Mushrooms (microwave)

SERVES 2 • PREP 15 min

INGREDIENTS

2 large potatoes

FOR THE FILLING

1 tablespoon oil
150g button mushrooms, sliced
125g soft cheese with garlic
salt and black pepper

METHOD

1 Prick the potatoes all over with a fork.

2 Place a kitchen towel on a microwaveable plate and put the potatoes on that.

3 Cook for 5 minutes, then turn the potatoes over and cook for another 5–6 minutes until they are tender.

4 Remove the potatoes from the paper (or they will stick) and let them stand for 2 minutes.

5 While the potatoes are cooking, prepare your filling.

6 Heat the oil in a pan and fry the mushrooms until they are soft and starting to brown.

7 Add the cheese and melt it down to a sauce, then season.

8 When the potatoes are ready, cut each one in half and pile on the filling.

Tuna-stuffed Jacket Potatoes (microwave)

SERVES 2 • PREP 20 min

INGREDIENTS

2 baking potatoes

FOR THE FILLING
1 tablespoon oil

1 small onion, chopped

1 clove garlic, crushed

*185g can tuna, drained and
  broken into chunks*

50g soft cheese

salt and black pepper

30g Cheddar cheese, grated

METHOD

1 Prick the potatoes all over with a fork.

2 Place a kitchen towel on a microwaveable plate and put the potatoes on that.

3 Cook for 5 minutes, then turn the potatoes over and cook for another 5–6 minutes until they are tender.

4 Remove the potatoes from the paper (or they will stick) and let them stand for 2 minutes.

5 While the potatoes are cooking, prepare your filling.

(continued over)

6 Heat the oil in a pan and fry the onion and garlic until they are soft and starting to brown at the edges.

7 Remove the pan from the heat and add the tuna and soft cheese. Season well.

8 Halve the potatoes and spoon out the flesh.

9 Mix the potato with the onion and garlic, tuna and soft cheese.

10 Place the potato skin shells on a microwaveable dish and stuff with the filling, cover with the grated cheese and microwave until the cheese melts.

VEGGIE DISHES

Student Standby

SERVES 1 • PREP 10 min

INGREDIENTS

1 tablespoon oil
1 onion, chopped
1 clove garlic, crushed (optional)
100g mushrooms, sliced
1 tomato, cut into wedges
25g cheese, grated
salt and black pepper

METHOD

1 Heat the oil in a pan and fry the onion, garlic (if using) and mushrooms until they are soft and starting to brown.

2 Add the tomato and cook for a few minutes until it begins to soften.

3 Stir in the cheese, season and serve.

TIP Use this as a topping for pasta or baked potatoes.

Veggie Varsity Pie

When *Grub on a Grant* was first published, my Varsity Pie was one of the first recipes to prove popular. This is the veggie version.

SERVES 1 • PREP 5 min • COOKING 20 min

INGREDIENTS

125g can condensed mushroom soup
100g can sweetcorn
100g can beans, any type
2 slices wholemeal bread, buttered
25g cheese, grated

METHOD

1 Preheat the oven to 200°C/400°F/Gas 6.

2 Mix together the soup, sweetcorn and beans and put them into a small casserole dish.

3 Halve the bread and place it, buttered side up, on top of the mixture.

4 Sprinkle with the grated cheese and bake in the preheated oven for 20 minutes.

Mushroom Stroganoff

SERVES 2 • PREP 15 min

INGREDIENTS

2 tablespoons oil
1 onion, thinly sliced
250g chestnut mushrooms, sliced
1 tablespoon wholegrain mustard
125ml crème fraîche
salt and black pepper

METHOD

1 Heat the oil in a pan and fry the onion until it is soft and starting to brown.

2 Add the mushrooms and fry for a few minutes until they are soft and starting to brown.

3 Stir in the mustard and crème fraîche and just heat through.

4 Season and serve.

TIP This is delicious served with rice but also works well with pasta or jacket potato.

Creamy Courgettes and Walnuts

SERVES 2 • PREP 15 min

INGREDIENTS

2 tablespoons oil
2 courgettes, cut into matchsticks
1 celery stick, trimmed and cut into matchsticks
1 onion, chopped
125g soft cheese with garlic
50g walnut pieces
salt and black pepper

METHOD

1 Heat the oil in a pan and fry the vegetables for a few minutes until they are soft and starting to brown.

2 Add the cheese and melt it down to a sauce.

3 Stir in the walnuts.

4 Season and serve.

TIP   Use this as a topping for pasta or baked potatoes.

Pipérade

SERVES 2 • PREP 20 min

INGREDIENTS

3 tablespoons oil
2 onions, thinly sliced
1 red pepper, thinly sliced
1 green pepper, thinly sliced
2 cloves garlic, crushed
salt and pepper
4 eggs, beaten

METHOD

1 Gently heat the oil in a pan and fry the vegetables with the garlic for a few minutes until they are softening and starting to brown at the edges.

2 Season the eggs and add them to the pan.

3 Cook over a low heat, stirring gently to allow the eggs to set.

TIP This is great served with a green salad and crusty French bread or ciabatta. You can make it for one person: halve the ingredients and substitute just 1 red pepper for the mixed peppers.

Veggies in Cheese Sauce

This is a useful recipe for a quick supper. Sometimes I add a little cream to the sauce and serve it with crusty French bread.

SERVES 1–2 • PREP 15 min

INGREDIENTS

150g cauliflower florets
100g carrots, sliced
50g frozen peas
1 tablespoon butter or margarine
1 tablespoon plain flour
1 teaspoon French mustard
125ml milk
50g cheese, grated

METHOD

1 Cook the cauliflower and carrots in boiling water for 7 minutes.

2 Add the peas and continue to cook for 3 minutes. Drain the vegetables.

3 Meanwhile, make the sauce. Melt the butter or margarine in a small pan, remove from the heat, stir in the flour and mustard, and gradually add just enough milk to make a smooth sauce.

4 Return the pan to the heat and, as the sauce thickens, add the remaining milk, stirring all the time.

5 Cook for 1 minute, and then add the cheese.

6 Mix with the cooked vegetables.

7 Serve with rice or pasta.

Cheesy Rice (microwave)

SERVES 1 • PREP 15 min + STANDING TIME

INGREDIENTS

knob of butter
½ small onion, finely chopped
½ red pepper, deseeded and flesh chopped
1 clove garlic, crushed
50g basmati rice
150ml vegetable stock
200g can chopped tomatoes
25g Cheddar cheese, grated,
  plus extra to serve
salt and pepper

METHOD

1 Put the butter, onion, pepper and garlic in a microwaveable bowl, cover and cook for 2 minutes.

2 Add the rice, stir, re-cover and cook for 1 minute.

3 Add the stock and tomatoes, stir, re-cover and cook for 10 minutes or until the rice is cooked.

4 Add the cheese and season.

5 Let the rice stand for 2 minutes.

6 Serve with extra cheese sprinkled on top.

Hot 'n' Spicy Vegetable Couscous

SERVES 2 • PREP 15 min

INGREDIENTS

100ml water
pinch of salt
pinch of cayenne pepper
4 tablespoons olive oil
100g couscous
1 small onion, chopped
1 green pepper, diced
2 tomatoes, deseeded and flesh chopped
1 chilli, deseeded and finely chopped
1 tablespoon lemon juice
salt and pepper

METHOD

1 In a medium saucepan, bring the water, salt, cayenne pepper and 1 tablespoon of oil to the boil.

2 Stir in the couscous, return to the boil, then cover and turn off the heat.

3 Heat another tablespoon of oil in a frying pan and gently fry the vegetables, including the chilli.

4 Stir the couscous, then cover again with the lid to let it finish cooking.

5 When the vegetables have cooked, stir the couscous once more to separate the grains, then mix in the cooked vegetables, the rest of the olive oil and the lemon juice. Season and serve.

Cheese and Tomato Vegetables

This is a really useful recipe to master as it is very easy and cheap.

SERVES 1 • PREP 15 min

INGREDIENTS

2 tablespoons oil
1 onion, chopped
2 cloves garlic, chopped
100g mushrooms, sliced
1 small courgette, quartered and sliced
3 tomatoes, quartered and sliced
2 tablespoons tomato purée
25g cheese, grated
salt and pepper

METHOD

1 Heat the oil in a pan and fry the onion, garlic, mushrooms and courgette for 5 minutes.

2 Add the tomatoes and tomato purée and cook for a further 3 minutes.

3 Stir in the cheese and season.

4 Serve with pasta or as a topping for baked potatoes.

Rice, Potatoes and Onions

Although this is a recipe for when you are utterly broke, don't wait until then to try it. It's really very good. When you're in the money, add some mango or lime chutney.

SERVES 1 • PREP 15 min

INGREDIENTS

200g potatoes, diced
oil for frying
100g rice
1 onion, sliced
1 teaspoon sugar
soy sauce

METHOD

1 Fry the potatoes in the oil while cooking the rice.

2 When the potatoes start to colour, add the onion and continue frying until both are browned.

3 Add the sugar and a dash of soy sauce. (This will make the vegetables slightly sticky as the sugar caramelises.)

4 When the rice is ready, arrange it on a plate and pour the caramelised vegetables over it.

Chilli and Garlic Beans

SERVES 1 • PREP 15 min

INGREDIENTS

1 tablespoon oil
1 onion, thinly sliced
1 chilli, deseeded and finely chopped
35g soft cheese with garlic
400g can economy red kidney beans,
  drained

METHOD

1 Heat the oil in a pan and fry the onion until it is soft
   and starting to brown.

2 Add the rest of the ingredients and continue cooking
   until the cheese melts down to a sauce.

TIP   Serve over pasta, with rice, a baked potato or on toast.

Beer Fondue

My brother introduced me to this version and it is now just as popular as our original wine-based fondue. I like to use Ruddles beer, but I'm sure whichever your favourite beer is will do! It's a strange thing that, considering how popular fondue sets used to be (almost *de rigueur* on wedding lists), I don't know many people who actually cook fondues. If you're lucky, you may be able to borrow one from your parents' cupboard – after all, if they never use it, why not let you have it? Otherwise car boot sales and ebay are good places to obtain a set.

SERVES 2 • PREP 15 min

INGREDIENTS

250ml beer

250g cheese, grated

1 clove garlic, crushed

1 tablespoon cornflour,
  mixed with a little cold water

25g butter

1 teaspoon French mustard

French bread, cubed, to serve

METHOD

1 Place the beer, cheese and garlic in a fondue pan or saucepan.

2 Heat gently until the cheese melts.

3 Add the cornflour mixture, butter and mustard.

4 Keep stirring until the fondue thickens and bubbles.

5 Serve in bowls if you do not have a fondue set that will keep the fondue warm while you eat, with French bread to dip into the fondue.

Cheese Fondue

This is very popular in our house – and we've finally met another couple that are just as fanatical about fondues as we are. We're in full agreement with you, Luigi and Donna – winter is most definitely the fondue season! Double the ingredients for a supper party dish for 4.

SERVES 2 • PREP 15 min

INGREDIENTS

200ml dry white wine

150g Gruyère, grated

150g Emmental, grated

1 teaspoon cornflour

2 tablespoons kirsch, vodka or gin

large fresh baguette or
*   sourdough loaf, cut into big chunks*

METHOD

1 Heat the wine in a large saucepan or fondue pot.

2 Add the cheeses.

3 Cook for a few minutes, stirring constantly, until the cheeses melt.

4 Blend the cornflour with the kirsch, vodka or gin and add it to the mixture, continuing to stir until the fondue thickens.

5 Serve at the table in the fondue pot or in bowls with chunks of crusty bread to dip into the fondue.

PASTA DISHES

Sun-dried Tomato Risotto

SERVES 1 • PREP 20 min

INGREDIENTS

1 tablespoon oil
1 small onion, chopped
65g risotto rice
250ml vegetable stock
25g Parmesan cheese, grated
8 sun-dried tomatoes, chopped or sliced
black pepper

METHOD

1 Gently heat the oil in a pan and fry the onion until it browns.

2 Add the rice and gently stir-fry for 1 minute until it is coated with oil.

3 Add ⅓ of the stock.

4 Gently cook until this stock is absorbed, then add half the remaining stock.

5 When this, too, is absorbed, add the remaining stock.

(continued over)

6 When all the stock has been absorbed, the rice should be cooked through and have a creamy consistency. (You can add more stock if you think it needs it – but don't overcook it.)

7 Stir in the cheese and tomatoes, and season with pepper.

TIP   Risotto is even better if you stir in a little butter just before serving it.

Quick Fried Cheese 'n' Tomato Pizza

SERVES 1 • PREP 20 min

INGREDIENTS

150g self-raising flour
pinch of salt
1 tablespoon oil, plus extra for greasing
90ml warm water
2 tablespoons tomato purée
sprinkling of oregano
1 tomato, sliced
25g cheese, grated

METHOD

1 Preheat the grill.

2 Mix the flour, salt and oil together with enough warm water to make a dough.

3 Knead for a couple of minutes until the dough is pliable.

4 Grease a large frying pan lightly with oil.

5 Press out the dough to fill the pan.

6 Fry for 4 minutes, then turn the dough and fry the other side.

7 Spread with the tomato purée, sprinkle the oregano over it, and top with the tomato slices and cheese.

8 Grill until the cheese melts and is bubbling.

(continued over)

QUICK FRIED CHEESE 'N' MUSHROOM PIZZA

Substitute 100g mushrooms for the tomato. Gently fry the mushrooms in some butter before starting to make the pizza, then cook as above.

Dolcelatte-dressed Spaghetti and Leeks

SERVES 2 • PREP 15 min

INGREDIENTS

175g spaghetti
1 tablespoon oil
1 leek, sliced
75g Dolcelatte cheese, diced
100g soft cheese
salt and black pepper

METHOD

1 Cook the spaghetti in boiling water according to the packet instructions.

2 While the spaghetti is cooking, heat the oil in a pan and fry the leek until it is soft and starting to brown.

3 Add the cheeses and stir while they blend into a smooth sauce.

4 Drain the spaghetti.

5 Season and stir the sauce into the spaghetti.

6 Serve immediately.

Pasta and Mushrooms with Hummus Sauce

SERVES 1 • PREP 20 min

INGREDIENTS

75g pasta
oil for frying
1 small onion, chopped
1 clove garlic, chopped
100g mushrooms, sliced
100g hummus
1 tablespoon milk
salt and pepper

METHOD

1 Add your chosen pasta to a saucepan of boiling water.

2 While it's cooking (about 10–12 minutes), make the sauce.

3 Heat the oil in a pan and fry the onion and garlic until they start to colour.

4 Add the mushrooms and continue to cook until they are soft.

5 Stir in the hummus and milk.

6 Cover and simmer gently for a few minutes.

7 When the pasta is cooked, drain it.

8 Season the sauce and serve it with the cooked, drained pasta.

Avocado and Banana with Pasta

This is a particular favourite of mine. It is full of calories, but very easy to make and very tasty.

SERVES 1 • PREP 20 min

INGREDIENTS

75g pasta
1 tablespoon soft butter or margarine
1 tablespoon smooth peanut butter
1 ripe avocado, peeled, stoned and chopped
1 ripe banana, chopped
black pepper

METHOD

1 Cook the pasta in boiling water until 'al dente' (cooked but still retaining some 'bite').

2 Beat together the butter or margarine and peanut butter.

3 When the pasta is cooked, drain it and add all the other ingredients.

4 Season with black pepper.

5 Return to the heat briefly to warm the ingredients through.

6 Serve immediately.

Tomato Provençale and Spaghetti

SERVES 1 • PREP 15 min

INGREDIENTS

75g spaghetti
200g can plum tomatoes
2 tablespoons oil
2 mushrooms, sliced
1 clove garlic, crushed
pinch of mixed herbs

METHOD

1 Cook the spaghetti in boiling water.

2 Drain the tomatoes, reserving half the juice, and chop them roughly.

3 Heat the oil in a pan and fry the tomatoes, mushrooms and garlic.

4 Add the reserved juice and herbs and simmer until the spaghetti is ready.

5 Drain the spaghetti, pour the sauce over it and serve.

Mushroom and Hazelnut Sauce (for Pasta)

SERVES 1 • PREP 15 min

INGREDIENTS

2 tablespoons oil
1 onion, chopped
1 clove garlic, crushed
100g mushrooms, sliced
1 teaspoon tomato purée
1 tablespoon roasted chopped hazelnuts
2 tablespoons crème fraîche
3 tablespoons water
salt and pepper

METHOD

1 Heat the oil in a pan and fry the onion, garlic and mushrooms until soft.

2 Add the tomato purée, hazelnuts, crème fraîche and water.

3 Stir until the sauce has heated through, season and serve with pasta.

Pasta with Creamy Salmon Sauce

SERVES 1 • PREP 20 min

INGREDIENTS

75g pasta
½ small onion, finely chopped
1 teaspoon butter or oil
100g can pink salmon, drained
small pinch of paprika
60ml double cream
1 teaspoon tomato ketchup
salt and pepper

METHOD

1 Cook the pasta as directed on the packet.

2 Meanwhile, fry the onion in the butter or oil until soft.

3 Stir in the rest of the ingredients, season and quickly heat through.

4 Serve over the cooked, drained pasta.

Tuna and Green Pepper Sauce and Pasta

SERVES 2 • PREP 20 min

INGREDIENTS

150g pasta
2 tablespoons olive oil
1 small onion, finely chopped
1 green pepper, deseeded and finely chopped
200g can tuna, drained
150ml double cream
salt and pepper

METHOD

1 Cook the pasta as directed on the packet.

2 Meanwhile, heat the oil and fry the onion and pepper until they start to soften and colour a little (about 5 minutes).

3 Add the drained tuna and cream and stir well.

4 Cook until the tuna is warmed through.

5 Season to taste and serve over the cooked, drained pasta.

Spaghetti Carbonara

SERVES 1 • PREP 15 min

INGREDIENTS

85g cubed pancetta
½ tablespoon olive oil
80g spaghetti
1 egg yolk, beaten
2 tablespoons double cream
1 tablespoon Parmesan cheese,
  freshly grated, plus extra to serve
salt and pepper

METHOD

1 Fry the pancetta in the oil for a few minutes until it is light brown and starting to crisp.

2 Put the pancetta on some kitchen paper and leave it to cool.

3 Cook the spaghetti as directed on the packet.

4 When cooked, drain the spaghetti, reserving a little of the cooking water.

5 Return the drained spaghetti to the pan.

6 Mix together the egg yolk, double cream, the cooled pancetta and the Parmesan.

7 Season well and mix the sauce into the spaghetti. If the sauce is slightly thick, add a little of the reserved cooking water to slacken it.

8 Serve immediately with some extra Parmesan.

Spaghetti Tricolor

SERVES 2 • PREP 15 min

INGREDIENTS

175g spaghetti
2 heaped tablespoons crème fraîche
1 clove garlic, crushed
2 sun-dried tomatoes, sliced
fresh basil, shredded
salt and black pepper
40g Parmesan or other hard cheese, cut into slivers

METHOD

1 Cook the spaghetti in a pan of boiling water as directed on the packet.

2 Meanwhile, mix together the rest of the ingredients except the Parmesan in a bowl, then season.

3 When the spaghetti is cooked, drain it well and return it to the pan with the sauce ingredients.

4 Warm it through and serve topped with the Parmesan.

TIP   Use a potato peeler to cut fine slivers of cheese for this recipe.

Spaghetti Putanesca

SERVES 2 • PREP 15 min

INGREDIENTS

200g spaghetti
1 tablespoon olive oil
1 onion, chopped
2 cloves garlic, crushed
1 tablespoon capers
200g can chopped tomatoes
50g stoned black olives
50g can anchovies in oil,
   drained and roughly chopped

METHOD

1 Cook the spaghetti in a pan of boiling water as directed on the the packet.

2 Heat the oil and fry the onion and garlic for a few minutes until they start to brown.

3 Add the remaining ingredients, cover tightly and simmer for 10 minutes.

4 When the spaghetti is cooked, drain it and serve topped with the sauce.

TIP This is a very gutsy sauce. If the flavours are too strong for you, try cooking it without the anchovies and adding the olives just before serving.

Pasta Alfredo

SERVES 2 • PREP 15 min

INGREDIENTS

160g pasta (fettuccine or tagliatelle
  is traditionally used in this dish)
50g butter
75ml double cream
50g Parmesan cheese, freshly grated,
  plus extra to serve
salt and pepper

METHOD

1 Bring a large pan of water to the boil and cook the pasta
  as directed on the packet.

2 Three minutes before the cooking time is up, melt the
  butter in another pan, then add the cream and
  Parmesan and simmer gently until the pasta is ready.
  Season well.

3 Drain the pasta and coat it with the cream sauce.

4 Serve immediately with extra Parmesan to taste.

Pasta with Walnuts

SERVES 2 • PREP 15 min

INGREDIENTS

150g pasta bows or tagliatelle
25g butter
100g mushrooms, sliced
80g Boursin, garlic and herb flavoured
60ml milk
50g chopped walnuts
salt and pepper

METHOD

1 Cook the pasta as directed on the packet.

2 Meanwhile, melt the butter in a pan and fry the mushrooms for 2–3 minutes.

3 Add the Boursin and milk to the pan and gently melt it down to make a sauce.

4 Add the walnuts and heat through.

5 Season well, then serve with the pasta.

Creamed Leek and Courgette Sauce (for Pasta)

SERVES 1 • PREP 15 min

INGREDIENTS

1 tablespoon oil
1 small leek, thinly sliced
1 small courgette, thinly sliced
40g soft cheese with garlic
black pepper

METHOD

1 Heat the oil in a pan and fry the leek and courgette until they are soft and starting to brown.

2 Add the cheese and melt it down until you have a creamy sauce.

3 Season with pepper and serve on your favourite pasta.

BROCCOLI SAUCE (FOR PASTA)

Just substitute an onion for the leek and 225g cooked broccoli for the courgette in the recipe above.

Spaghetti Tunagnese

SERVES 2 • PREP 15 min

INGREDIENTS

150g spaghetti
142ml carton single cream
25g Cheddar cheese, finely grated
100g can tuna, drained and flaked
salt
Worcestershire sauce, to taste
  (optional)
½ bunch of spring onions, chopped

METHOD

1 Cook the spaghetti in a large saucepan of boiling water as directed on the packet, then drain it.

2 Meanwhile, put the cream in a small milk pan and bring it to the boil, then gently simmer for 5 minutes.

3 Take the cream off the heat and add the cheese, blending well to make a smooth sauce.

4 Add the rest of the ingredients and heat through gently.

5 Serve with the cooked spaghetti.

TIP This is even more delicious if topped with shavings of Parmesan cheese (use a potato peeler) and some freshly ground black pepper.

Pasta Frittata

SERVES 1 • PREP 15 min

INGREDIENTS

1 tablespoon oil
1 small onion, chopped
1 clove garlic, crushed
25g cooked pasta
2 eggs, beaten
25g cheese, grated

METHOD

1 Preheat the grill.

2 Heat the oil in a medium frying pan or omelette pan.

3 Gently fry the onion and garlic for 5 minutes.

4 Add the pasta and stir well.

5 Pour in the eggs and sprinkle over the cheese.

6 Cook for a few minutes until the bottom of the frittata has set.

7 Finish off under the grill; the frittata is done when it is golden brown and puffed up.

8 Serve with a green vegetable or salad.

Spaghetti with Anchovies and Garlic Crumbs

SERVES 2 • PREP 15 min

INGREDIENTS

160g spaghetti
knob of butter
50g can anchovies – reserve oil, chop anchovies
2 cloves garlic, crushed
1 slice bread, crumbed
squeeze of lemon juice (optional)
black pepper
Parmesan cheese, freshly grated, to serve (optional)

METHOD

1 Bring a pan of water to the boil and cook the spaghetti as directed on the packet.

2 In a small pan, melt the butter and add the anchovies and garlic and cook for 2 minutes very gently. The anchovies will melt into the butter.

3 Add the breadcrumbs, stir well and then turn off the heat.

4 When the spaghetti is cooked, drain it and mix with the anchovy and garlic crumbs.

5 Drizzle with a little of the reserved oil from the anchovy tin.

6 Squeeze over the lemon (if using), season and serve topped with Parmesan, if you wish.

Pasta with Tomato and Garlic

SERVES 1 • PREP 15 min

INGREDIENTS

100g pasta
knob of butter or margarine
1 tablespoon tomato purée
1 clove garlic, crushed

METHOD

1   Cook the pasta in a pan of boiling water as directed on the packet, then drain.

2   Return the pasta to the pan, add the other ingredients and heat through.

Pasta with Cheese 'n' Garlic Sauce

SERVES 1 • PREP 15 min

INGREDIENTS

75g pasta
1 tablespoon oil
1 onion, diced
3 tablespoons milk
75g soft cheese, herb and garlic flavoured
salt and pepper

METHOD

1 Cook the pasta in a pan of boiling water as directed on the packet.

2 Meanwhile, heat the oil in another pan and fry the onion until it is soft and starting to brown at the edges.

3 Add the milk and cheese and stir until it melts and makes a sauce.

4 Drain the cooked pasta and mix with the sauce. Season and serve.

STIR-FRIES AND CURRIES

Thai Prawns

SERVES 2 • PREP 15 min

INGREDIENTS

1 tablespoon oil
300g packet frozen raw jumbo prawns
1 teaspoon minced ginger
1 clove garlic, crushed
2 teaspoons Thai red curry paste
1 tablespoon soy sauce

METHOD

1 Heat the oil in a frying pan.

2 Add all the ingredients and stir-fry for 5 minutes.

3 Make sure that the prawns have all turned pink and are cooked through before serving.

TIP Serve with rice or noodles.

Stir-fried Beef in Oyster Sauce

SERVES 1 • PREP 15 min

INGREDIENTS

1 teaspoon sesame seeds

1 tablespoon oil

125g thin cut frying steak, cut into thin slices

125g mixed vegetables, e.g. broccoli, mushrooms, peppers and spring onions, sliced

½ tablespoon soy sauce

150g sachet ready-to-use noodles

2–3 tablespoons oyster sauce

METHOD

1 Dry-fry the sesame seeds in a frying pan or wok until they start to darken.

2 Remove them from the pan.

3 Heat the oil in the pan and then add the beef. Quickly fry it for just a minute or two – the beef should not be totally cooked through at this stage or it will be tough.

4 Remove it from the pan.

5 Add the vegetables and stir-fry them for 2 minutes.

6 Add the soy sauce and continue stir-frying until the vegetables are cooked.

7 Return the beef to the pan with its juices and add the noodles and oyster sauce.

8 Stir well. Cook until the noodles have heated through and then stir in the sesame seeds and serve.

Chilli Vegetables and Noodles

SERVES 1 • PREP 20 min

INGREDIENTS

2 tablespoons oil
1 onion, sliced
1 large carrot, peeled and cut into matchsticks
100g mushrooms, thickly sliced
100g green beans, halved or sliced
85g packet dried noodles, vegetable flavour
200ml boiling water
1 tablespoon minced chilli

METHOD

1 Heat the oil in a pan and fry the onion for 3–4 minutes.

2 Add the other vegetables and stir-fry for 2 minutes.

3 Break up the noodles, then add them to the pan with the water and the contents of the flavouring sachet.

4 Stir well, cover and simmer for 3 minutes.

5 Stir in the chilli and serve.

TIP Alter the amount of chilli to suit your own taste. You can also use pre-cooked noodles with a little oyster sauce or tomato ketchup mixed with some water and soy sauce instead of the dried noodles and boiling water.

Thai Lamb

SERVES 2 • PREP 20 min

INGREDIENTS

1 tablespoon oil
1 onion, chopped
2 cloves garlic, crushed
2 teaspoons minced ginger
150g lamb neck fillet, thinly sliced
100g mushrooms, sliced
½ bunch of spring onions, sliced
1 teaspoon minced chilli
1 tablespoon soy sauce
1 teaspoon runny honey or demerara sugar

METHOD

1 Heat the oil in a pan and fry the onion, garlic and ginger for 4 minutes.

2 Add the lamb and cook for another 4 minutes.

3 Add the rest of the ingredients and stir-fry for another 2 minutes.

TIP   This is really good with rice and more soy sauce for serving.

Quick-fix Chicken Noodles

SERVES 2 • PREP 20 min

INGREDIENTS

2 tablespoons oil
1 onion, sliced
1 chicken breast, sliced
1 green pepper, deseeded and sliced
100g broccoli florets
1 teaspoon minced ginger (optional)
100g packet dried noodles, chow mein flavour
250ml boiling water
1 tablespoon soy sauce

METHOD

1 Heat the oil in a pan and fry the onion for 3 minutes until it starts to brown.

2 Add the chicken and stir-fry for another 3 minutes.

3 Add the pepper, broccoli and ginger (if using), then stir-fry for 2 minutes.

4 Break up the noodles and add them to the pan with the water and the contents of the flavouring packet.

5 Stir, cover and cook for 3–4 minutes or until the water is nearly absorbed.

6 Stir in the soy sauce and serve.

TIP Serve with rice and more soy sauce. You can substitute other flavoured noodles to vary this recipe.

Chinese Rice with Omelette

SERVES 1 • PREP 20 min

INGREDIENTS

100g basmati rice
250ml vegetable stock
25g butter
50g mushrooms, sliced
1 tablespoon frozen peas
3 spring onions, chopped
1 egg, beaten
1 tablespoon milk
salt and pepper
1 tablespoon soy sauce

METHOD

1 Put the rice and stock in a saucepan and bring to the boil. Cover and simmer for 10–12 minutes until all the stock has been absorbed.

2 Meanwhile, melt half the butter and stir-fry the mushrooms, peas and spring onions for 3–4 minutes. Set aside.

3 Beat together the egg and milk, and season.

4 Melt the rest of the butter in a small frying pan and pour in the egg mixture. Swirl the egg over the bottom of the pan. Draw back the edges of the omelette from the sides of the pan so that any uncooked egg can run underneath.

5 When the egg has set, slide the omelette on to a plate, roll it up and cut it into little egg rolls.

6 When the rice is cooked, add the soy sauce and mix in the stir-fried vegetables.

7 Put in a bowl and serve with the egg rolls on top.

TIP I like this served with Quick Chilli 'n' Tomato Sauce (page 342).

Sweet 'n' Sour Chicken and Rice Dish (microwave)

SERVES 1 • PREP 15 min + STANDING TIME

INGREDIENTS

1 chicken breast fillet, skinless, sliced thinly
50g basmati rice
red pepper, deseeded and flesh chopped
2 slices pineapple, from a can, chopped into chunks
juice of ½ lemon
1 tablespoon pineapple juice from can
1 tablespoon soy sauce
1 tablespoon tomato ketchup
100ml water
pepper

METHOD

1 Put all the ingredients in a microwaveable dish, cover and cook for 5 minutes.

2 Stir.

3 Cook again for 5 minutes.

4 Let it stand for 5 minutes.

Chinese Vegetables and Noodles (microwave)

SERVES 2 • PREP 15 min

INGREDIENTS

2 x 50g nests medium egg noodles
1 tablespoon oil
300g pack prepared Chinese stir-fry vegetables
1 teaspoon sesame oil
2 tablespoons oyster sauce
2 tablespoons tomato ketchup
2 tablespoons soy sauce
1 tablespoon runny honey

METHOD

1 Place the noodles in a microwaveable dish, cover with boiling water then cover with a lid or some clingfilm pierced a few times and cook for 2 minutes.

2 Drain and remove from the dish.

3 Add the oil and the prepared vegetables to the dish and stir well.

4 Cover and cook for 3 minutes.

(continued over)

5 Mix the sesame oil into the noodles, making sure that they do not stick together.

6 Mix the rest of the ingredients together in a small bowl.

7 When the vegetables have cooked, add the sauce and noodles to the dish, stir well and cook for 1 minute. Serve.

TIP I like to serve this with some crushed nuts to add protein to the dish. Or you could throw in some cooked chicken.

Thai Noodles

SERVES 2 • PREP 15 min

INGREDIENTS

2 x 50g nests medium egg noodles
2 tablespoons oil
1 large carrot, cut into matchsticks
100g baby corn, halved lengthways
150g asparagus tips or green beans, cut into lengths
1 teaspoon minced ginger
2 cloves garlic, crushed
½ red chilli, deseeded and finely chopped
several spring onions, thinly sliced into lengths
2 tablespoons soy sauce
1 tablespoon lime juice
1 teaspoon sugar

METHOD

1 Put the nests in a pan of boiling water and cook for 2 minutes. Drain.

2 Heat the oil in a large frying pan or wok and quickly stir-fry the vegetables for 2 minutes.

3 Add the rest of the ingredients and the cooked noodles and stir-fry for 2 minutes.

Sweet 'n' Sour Vegetables

SERVES 2 • PREP 15 min

INGREDIENTS

2 tablespoons oil
½ green pepper, sliced
½ red pepper, sliced
1 carrot, cut into matchsticks
2 celery sticks, sliced
½ x 225g can bamboo shoots, drained
160g jar sweet 'n' sour sauce

METHOD

1 Heat the oil in a large frying pan or wok and stir-fry the peppers, carrot and celery for 2–3 minutes.

2 Add the bamboo shoots and sweet 'n' sour sauce.

3 Cook for 2 minutes and serve with noodles or rice.

Chicken Chow Mein

SERVES 2 • PREP 15 min

INGREDIENTS

1 tablespoon oil
1 large chicken breast, sliced finely
1 red pepper, deseeded and chopped
1 teaspoon minced ginger
1 clove garlic, crushed
2 x 150g medium cooked noodles
2 tablespoons soy sauce
1 teaspoon Chinese five spice powder
½ bunch of spring onions, chopped
dash of sesame seed oil, to serve (optional)

METHOD

1 Heat the oil and stir-fry the chicken for a few minutes until starting to brown. Add the pepper, ginger and garlic.

2 Stir-fry for 3–4 minutes before adding the rest of the ingredients.

3 Cook for a few minutes to heat through.

4 Add a dash of sesame seed oil, if using, just before serving.

TIP Sesame seed oil is a good store-cupboard ingredient as it adds a lot to Chinese dishes and keeps for a long time.
I've used pre-cooked noodles here but you can simmer 2 x 50g nests of medium egg noodles for 2 minutes, drain and add the sesame seed oil (which prevents them from sticking together). You can also add a little sweet chilli sauce to this dish.

Vegetable Chow Mein

SERVES 2 • PREP 10 min

INGREDIENTS

2 x 50g nests medium egg noodles
2 tablespoons oil
100g button mushrooms, cleaned
50g frozen peas

FOR THE SAUCE

2 tablespoons soy sauce
1 clove garlic, crushed or finely chopped
½ teaspoon Chinese five spice powder
1 tablespoon sweet chilli sauce
2 tablespoons tomato sauce

METHOD

1 Cook the noodles until soft, then drain them.

2 Toss in 1 tablespoon of the oil.

3 Stir-fry the mushrooms and peas in the remaining oil for 2 minutes.

4 Add the sauce ingredients and cook for 1 minute.

5 Add the noodles and stir through before serving.

Stir-fried Broccoli and Cashews

SERVES 2 • PREP 15 min

INGREDIENTS

1 tablespoon oil
200g broccoli florets, sliced
1 clove garlic, crushed
1 teaspoon minced ginger
50g unsalted cashews, dry-fried until brown

FOR THE SAUCE

1 teaspoon cornflour
4 tablespoons water
2 tablespoons soy sauce
2 tablespoons sherry or white wine
1 teaspoon honey

METHOD

1 Heat the oil a large frying pan or wok and stir-fry the broccoli, garlic and ginger for 2 minutes.

2 Add the cashews and stir through.

3 Dissolve the cornflour in the water.

4 Mix the cornflour with the other sauce ingredients and add the mixture to the pan.

5 Cook for 2 minutes. Serve.

Prawns in Lime Ginger Butter

SERVES 2 • PREP 15 min

INGREDIENTS

25g butter
1 onion, finely chopped
1 clove garlic, crushed (optional)
½ teaspoon minced ginger
200g king or tiger prawns, cooked
juice of 1 lime
crusty bread to serve

METHOD

1   Melt the butter in a frying pan.

2   Add the onion and fry gently until golden and soft.

3   Add the rest of the ingredients and cook gently until heated through.

4   Stir well and serve with crusty bread to mop up the juices.

TIP   Raw prawns can be used but make sure they are cooked through – they turn a pinky/red – before eating.

Egg and Lentil Curry

SERVES 2 • PREP 20 min

INGREDIENTS

3 eggs
1 tablespoon oil
1 onion, chopped
2 cloves garlic, crushed
2 tablespoons medium curry powder
200ml carton creamed coconut
400g can brown lentils, drained
1 tablespoon Indian chutney

METHOD

1 Place the eggs in a saucepan, cover with cold water and bring to the boil. Cook for 8–10 minutes.

2 Plunge the eggs into cold water to cool.

3 Peel off the shells and cut each in half lengthways.

4 While the eggs are cooking, heat the oil in a pan and fry the onion and garlic until they start to brown.

5 Add the curry powder and a little creamed coconut and blend into a sauce.

6 Add the rest of the coconut and the well-drained lentils.

7 Cook for a few minutes to thicken the sauce.

8 Stir in the chutney and serve the eggs on top of the lentils.

TIP   Serve with rice or chapattis.

Fish with Coconut Curry Relish (microwave)

SERVES 2 • PREP 15 min + STANDING TIME

INGREDIENTS

COCONUT CURRY RELISH

50g desiccated coconut

100ml milk

25g butter

½ small onion, finely chopped

1 tablespoon korma paste

1 large tomato, deseeded and flesh chopped

2 tablespoons natural yogurt, cream or crème fraîche

FOR THE FISH

2 x fish fillets (approx 100g each)

1 tablespoon lemon juice

METHOD

1 In a microwaveable bowl, mix the coconut and milk and then microwave for 1 minute; put to one side.

2 In another microwaveable bowl, melt the butter and then mix in the onion and korma paste. Cover and cook for 3 minutes.

3 Add the tomatoes to the onion mix and stir in the coconut milk. Cover and cook for 2 minutes.

4 Add the yogurt, cream or crème fraîche, mix well, cover and cook for 30 seconds. Stir and leave to stand for at least 5 minutes, before starting to cook the fish. (The longer the relish is left, the better it gets – it is even better made the day before.)

5 Put the fish on a microwaveable plate and sprinkle with lemon juice.

6 Cover and cook for 2–3 minutes.

7 Check after 2 minutes to see how cooked the fish is.

8 When the fish is cooked, serve it with the coconut curry relish.

Spicy Rice

SERVES 1 • PREP 20 min

INGREDIENTS

1 tablespoon oil
½ small onion, chopped
50g frozen peas (optional)
50g basmati rice
pinch each of garam masala, coriander,
    cayenne pepper, turmeric
knob of butter
½ pepper, diced
several mushrooms, sliced
1 clove garlic, crushed
½ red chilli, deseeded and finely chopped

METHOD

1 Heat the oil in a saucepan and add the onion and peas (if using).

2 Gently fry for 5 minutes.

3 Add the rice and spices and stir well.

4 Cover with boiling water and bring to the boil.

5 Cover, reduce the heat and simmer for 10 minutes.

6 Meanwhile, melt the butter and gently cook the pepper, mushrooms, garlic and chilli for a few minutes until soft.

7 When the rice is cooked, drain if necessary and then mix with the cooked vegetables.

MEAT DISHES

Barbecued Pork Chop

SERVES 1 • PREP 20 min

INGREDIENTS

1 pork chop
1 small onion, chopped
25g butter
1 tablespoon tomato ketchup
1 tablespoon vinegar
1 tablespoon brown sugar or honey
dash of soy sauce

METHOD

1 Fry the pork and onion in the butter for 15–18 minutes, turning the meat after 10 minutes. Cook thicker chops for the longer time.

2 Add the rest of the ingredients and cook for a couple of minutes.

Honey-glazed Lamb Steak

SERVES 1 • PREP 15 min

INGREDIENTS

15g butter
½ tablespoon runny honey
1 teaspoon mustard, Dijon or wholegrain
salt and pepper
1 medium lamb steak

METHOD

1 In a bowl, beat the butter until it is creamy, then add the honey and mustard, season and mix well.

2 Use this to cover the lamb steak.

3 Preheat the grill and then grill the lamb for 4–6 minutes on each side, basting with the cooking juices when turning the steak.

4 If you prefer your meat well cooked, cook it for the longer time.

Lamb in Mustard Cream Sauce

SERVES 2 • PREP 15 min

INGREDIENTS

25g butter
1 small onion, finely chopped
2 lean lamb steaks
1 teaspoon redcurrant jelly
1 teaspoon wholegrain mustard
2 tablespoons double cream

METHOD

1 In a frying pan, melt the butter and cook the onion for 5 minutes.

2 Add the steaks and cook them for 3 minutes on each side.

3 Add the redcurrant jelly, mustard and cream, and simmer gently until the jelly has melted into the sauce.

Microwave Chilli

SERVES 2 • PREP 15 min + STANDING TIME

INGREDIENTS

1 tablespoon oil

1 small onion, finely chopped

½ green pepper, deseeded and chopped

1 clove garlic, crushed

200–250g beef mince

3 tablespoons tomato purée

1 teaspoon mild chilli powder (use more if you like it spicier)

200g can red kidney beans, rinsed and drained

3 tablespoons of boiling water

METHOD

1 Place the oil, onion, pepper and garlic in a microwaveable dish.

2 Cover and cook for 2 minutes.

3 Add the mince and cook for 3 minutes.

4 Add all the other ingredients, including the water, and cook for 3 minutes.

5 Let it stand for 5 minutes.
This is great served with tacos or crusty bread.

MICROWAVE KEEMA CURRY

Substitute 1 tablespoon korma curry paste for the chilli powder and omit the red kidney beans. Serve with naans or rice.

Mince-stuffed Peppers (microwave)

SERVES 2 • PREP 20 min

INGREDIENTS

1 *red pepper, halved lengthways*
  and seeds removed
1 *tablespoon oil*
1 *small onion, finely chopped*
1 *clove garlic, crushed*
200–250g *beef mince*
2 *tomatoes, seeds removed and*
  flesh chopped
2 *tablespoons tomato purée*
pinch of oregano
salt and pepper
50g *Cheddar cheese, grated (optional)*

METHOD

1 Put the pepper cut side up in a shallow microwaveable dish.

2 Cover and cook for 3 minutes.

3 Remove from the oven.

4 Place the oil, onion and garlic in a microwaveable dish, cover and cook for 2 minutes.

5 Add the mince, stir, and cook for 3 minutes. Fork through thoroughly to break up lumps.

(continued over)

6 Add the chopped tomatoes, tomato purée and oregano, stir and cook for 3 minutes.

7 Remove and again fork through thoroughly.

8 Pile the mince mixture into the peppers, sprinkle with the cheese (if using) and cook for 1 minute, so that cheese is just melting.

3 Quick & Easy Food
cooking for 2 or more in under 30 minutes

Not all students who live in self-catering accommodation are in halls; many are in accommodation with a number of bedrooms that share a living space, kitchen and bathroom. (Some now even have en-suite bathrooms!) These shared accommodations do generally have a more homely feel to them and, even though you have not picked the people you are sharing with, it is not uncommon for these to be the very people you will strike up your initial friendships with, then perhaps go on to share accommodation with outside campus. Although most people don't cook and eat together every night, it is usually possible to cook together on some nights and a bonus is that it works out cheaper this way.

While at my old university, doing some research for this book, I dropped in at the students' union and picked up a uni handbook. In the intros to the union reps, more than half of them mentioned food when asked what would be involved in their ideal evening (the same proportion that mentioned alcohol as featuring in their ideal evening!).

If you are lucky enough to be living in shared accommodation off campus with friends, then this is where the fun starts. We had some great laughs while busily preparing meals. It's when people come together at the end of the day that you get to hear all the latest gossip, find out what's going on in the world, and learn what's planned for the evening and the weekend – and get the reports on what happened last night . . .

If you have nothing particular planned for an evening, why not invite a friend or two over for a meal? A leisurely meal followed by a trip to a bar was one of our favourite ways of spending the evening (winning hands down every time over *really* getting to grips with that essay).

If you are living in a communal household, although it is not usual to cook for everyone every night, it is common to have a kitty for some items, such as milk, bread, tea and coffee. (It is also common to have arguments about who's paid, who's finished the milk and so on!) If someone offers to cook one evening, the cost of the meal is divided among those taking part.

If you are living in a shared house, hopefully you will not have the problem of people nicking your foodstuffs (or at least they should be able to provide a plausible excuse as to why they did so!). You should therefore be able to make more use of fresh vegetables in your cooking. You will soon find that an added bonus is that it works out cheaper per head to cook in quantity.

THE CHOICES:

SOUPS AND SALADS

Cheese and Courgette Soup

Vichyssoise (Potato and Leek Soup)

Vegetable and Lentil Soup

Tuscan Bean Soup

Gado Gado Salad

Carrot, Egg and Olive Salad

Tomato and Mozzarella Salad

Roasted Pepper Salad

Niçoise Salad

Chilli-dressed Tuna and Roasted Pepper Salad

OTHER SNACKS

Egg and Vegetable Hash

Tuna Rice Medley

Greek Feta and Vegetable Casserole

Spanish Tortilla

Cheese Boreks

Mushrooms *à la Grecque*

Vegetables in Creamy Mustard Sauce with Chorizo

Tomato, Leek and Bacon Rice

Veggieburgers

PASTA DISHES

Risotto with Mushrooms and Walnuts

Risi e Bisi

Quick Pizza

Macaroni Cheese

Chorizo and Pepper Sauce (for Pasta)

Farfalle with Pepperoni and Olives

Pasta with Sausage Sauce

Spaghetti Bolognese

Veggie Spag Bol

Pasta with Roasted Veg

STIR-FRIES AND CURRIES

Thai Prawn Curry

Teriyaki Chicken Stir-fry

Vegetable Curry (microwave)

Coconut Chicken Curry

Vegetable Biryani

Saag Aloo (Spinach and Potato Curry)

MEAT DISHES

Baked Lemon Chicken

Chicken and Banana Creole

Sausages with Onion Gravy

Chicken Nachos

Tortilla-topped Mexican Pie

Chilli con Carne

Chicken Fajitas

SOUPS AND SALADS

Cheese and Courgette Soup

I tend to make cheese and vegetable soup in the winter; this soup is my summer version.

SERVES 2 • PREP 15 min • COOKING 15 min

INGREDIENTS

150g courgettes, cleaned and sliced
1 onion, chopped
1 medium potato, peeled and diced
500ml vegetable stock
100g Cheddar cheese, grated
salt and pepper

METHOD

1 Put the vegetables and stock in a medium saucepan and bring to the boil.

2 Cover and reduce the heat.

3 Simmer gently for 15 minutes

4 Stir in the cheese and continue to cook until it has melted.

5 Season and serve.

Vichyssoise (Potato and Leek Soup)

This is a useful recipe for a dinner party. If you have access to a blender or liquidiser, you can make it really special by adding a small tub of crème fraîche and liquidising. You will then have a smooth soup that can also be served cold – with an ice cube or two in the middle and garnished with chopped chives.

SERVES 2 • PREP 10 min • COOKING 20 min

INGREDIENTS

200g potatoes, diced
200g leeks, well washed and chopped
375ml vegetable stock
125ml milk
salt and pepper

METHOD

1 Put all the ingredients in a saucepan and bring to the boil.

2 Cover and simmer for 20 minutes until the vegetables are soft.

3 Check the seasoning and serve.

Vegetable and Lentil Soup

SERVES 4 • PREP 20 min • COOKING 25 min

INGREDIENTS

500g potatoes, peeled and diced
1 carrot, halved and sliced
1 onion, chopped
1.2 litres vegetable stock,
  made with 2 stock cubes and
  boiling water
400g can lentils, drained

METHOD

1 Put all the ingredients in a large saucepan and bring to the boil.

2 Cover and simmer for 25 minutes.

3 Squash some of the vegetables against the side of the saucepan to thicken the soup a little.

4 Serve with crusty bread.

Tuscan Bean Soup

SERVES 2 • PREP 10 min • COOKING 25 min

INGREDIENTS

1 tablespoon oil
1 small onion, finely chopped
1 clove garlic, crushed
1 large carrot, diced
1 stick celery, diced (optional)
400g can chopped tomatoes
1 tablespoon tomato purée
400g can cannellini, borlotti or
  flageolet beans, drained
500ml vegetable stock
salt and pepper

METHOD

1 Heat the oil in a medium saucepan and then add the onion, garlic, carrot and celery (if using), and gently fry for 5 minutes.

2 Add the rest of the ingredients and simmer gently for 20 minutes.

TIP When you are in the money, this is even nicer with some fresh herbs added – choose from rosemary, thyme, parsley or basil.

Gado Gado Salad

SERVES 4 • PREP 25 min

INGREDIENTS

FOR THE SALAD
4 eggs
1 iceberg lettuce, finely shredded
2 carrots, peeled and cut into fine shavings
½ cucumber, peeled and cut into matchsticks

FOR THE PEANUT DRESSING
4 tablespoons crunchy peanut butter
juice of 1 lime
½–1 tablespoon honey or sugar to taste
1 tablespoon soy sauce
½ teaspoon minced chilli

METHOD

1 Put the eggs in a saucepan, cover with cold water and bring to the boil.

2 Simmer for 10 minutes, then plunge the eggs into cold water to cool.

3 Peel off the shells and cut each egg in half lengthways.

4 Place the salad ingredients in a bowl.

5 Put all the peanut dressing ingredients in a pan and heat gently, stirring until they combine. Add honey or sugar until sweet enough for you.

6 Drizzle the dressing over the salad and serve immediately.

Carrot, Egg and Olive Salad

SERVES 4 • PREP 25 min

INGREDIENTS

4 eggs
800g carrots, grated
juice of ½ lemon
2 tablespoons black mustard seeds
3 tablespoons olive oil
200g mixed olives, drained
salt and black pepper

METHOD

1 Put the eggs in a saucepan, cover with cold water and bring to the boil.

2 Simmer for 10 minutes, then plunge the eggs into cold water to cool.

3 Peel off the shells and cut each egg in half lengthways.

4 Meanwhile, mix together the carrots, lemon juice and mustard seeds.

5 Heat the oil in a frying pan, add the carrot mixture and stir-fry until the carrot is just softening and the seeds begin to pop, then remove immediately.

6 Put the contents of the pan in the middle of a serving dish and surround with the egg halves and olives, before seasoning and serving.

TIP   Half the prep time of this dish is taken up by grating the carrots, so if you can get some help here you can save time.
Use the black mustard seeds to give a tang to other salads or use them up when cooking curries.

Tomato and Mozzarella Salad

SERVES 4 • PREP 10 min

INGREDIENTS

8 tomatoes, sliced
400g mozzarella cheese, sliced
4 tablespoons olive oil
2 tablespoons white wine vinegar
pinch of sugar
salt and black pepper

METHOD

1 Arrange alternate slices of tomato and cheese on each plate.

2 Put the rest of the ingredients in a screw-top jar and shake well.

3 Drizzle the dressing all over the salad.

TIP   This is a dish where the better the oil used, the better the finished dish.
If you are serving it with other dishes that use basil, keep back a few sprigs to garnish this salad.

Roasted Pepper Salad

SERVES 4 • PREP 15 min • COOKING 15 min

INGREDIENTS

8 red Romano peppers, deseeded
  and halved lengthways
2 cloves garlic, sliced thinly
2 tablespoons olive oil
50g can anchovy fillets in extra
  virgin oil, drained but oil reserved,
  fillets chopped
salt and black pepper

METHOD

1 Preheat the oven to 220°C/425°F/Gas 7.

2 Mix together all the ingredients and season.

3 Cover a shallow roasting tin with foil and spread the
   ingredients over this. Drizzle with the oil from the
   anchovies tin.

4 Roast in the preheated oven for 15 minutes, until the
   peppers are soft and just starting to blacken at the
   edges.

5 Transfer with all the juices from the roasting tin to a
   serving dish and serve with lots of crusty bread to mop
   up the juices.

Niçoise Salad

SERVES 4 • PREP 20 min

INGREDIENTS

FOR THE SALAD

4 eggs

12 tomatoes, cut into wedges

2 green peppers, deseeded and
  cut into thin rings

1 cucumber, peeled and thinly sliced

300g can broad beans, drained

2 x 185g cans tuna, drained and flaked

2 x 50g cans anchovy fillets, drained

200g black olives

FOR THE DRESSING

120ml olive oil

3 tablespoons white wine vinegar

2 cloves garlic, crushed

salt and pepper

METHOD

1 Put the eggs in a saucepan, cover with cold water and bring to the boil.

2 Simmer for 10 minutes, then plunge the eggs into cold water to cool.

3 Peel off the shells and cut each egg in half lengthways.

4 Arrange all the salad ingredients on a serving dish.

5 Put the oil, vinegar and garlic in a screw-top jar and season. Shake well, then pour over the salad.

TIP   I like anchovies a lot but if you think this might be too much, just use one can.

Chilli-dressed Tuna and Roasted Pepper Salad

SERVES 4 • PREP 25 min

INGREDIENTS

FOR THE SALAD

4 eggs
Roasted Pepper Salad (page 159)
2 x 185g cans tuna, drained and flaked
100g black olives
1 tablespoon capers

FOR THE DRESSING

4 tablespoons olive oil
1 tablespoon white wine vinegar
2 teaspoons minced chilli
2 cloves garlic, crushed
salt and pepper

METHOD

1 Put the eggs in a saucepan, cover with cold water and bring to the boil.

2 Simmer for 10 minutes, then plunge the eggs into cold water to cool.

3 Peel off the shells and cut each egg in half lengthways.

4 Pile all the salad ingredients on to a serving dish.

5 Put the dressing ingredients into a screw-top jar and shake well, then drizzle all over the salad.

OTHER SNACKS

Egg and Vegetable Hash

SERVES 2 • PREP 30 min

INGREDIENTS

1 tablespoon oil
200g new potatoes, diced
200g red and orange peppers, sliced
200g courgettes, halved and sliced
pinch of dried oregano
4–6 eggs (depending on appetite)
salt and pepper

METHOD

1   Heat the oil and fry the potatoes for 5 minutes and then add the other vegetables.

2   Continue to fry for 5 minutes, then add the oregano and carefully break the eggs over the vegetables.

3   Cover and cook for 3–5 minutes until the whites are cooked but the yolks still have a 'wobble'.

4   Season and divide between 2 plates to serve.

TIP   This is great with some bread and tomato ketchup or brown sauce.

Tuna Rice Medley

SERVES 4 • PREP 25 min

INGREDIENTS

2 tablespoons oil
1 onion, chopped
1 red pepper, deseeded and diced
1 clove garlic, crushed
250g basmati rice
700ml chicken stock
salt and black pepper
300g can sweetcorn, drained
1 bunch of spring onions, chopped
185g can tuna in spring water, drained

METHOD

1 Heat the oil in a large frying pan and fry the onion,
   pepper and garlic until they are soft and starting to
   brown.

2 Stir in the rice, then add the stock.

3 Season and cook, stirring occasionally, until the rice is
   cooked and has absorbed the stock – about 10–15
   minutes.

4 Stir in the rest of the ingredients and serve.

TIP   We like this served with either a sweet chilli sauce or smoky
        barbecue sauce.

Greek Feta and Vegetable Casserole

SERVES 1 • PREP 15 min • COOKING 15 min

INGREDIENTS

4 tablespoons olive oil

1 large onion, thinly sliced into rings

3 peppers of mixed colours,
   deseeded, halved and cut into
   half circles

4 cloves garlic, crushed

4 tomatoes, chopped

200g feta cheese, cubed

1 teaspoon oregano

black pepper

METHOD

1 Preheat the oven to 200°C/400°F/Gas 6.

2 Heat 3 tablespoons of the oil and fry the onion, peppers and garlic until they are soft and starting to brown.

3 Add the tomatoes and cook for a few more minutes to soften.

4 Transfer to an ovenproof dish and mix in the feta and oregano.

5 Season with black pepper, drizzle with the remaining oil, cover tightly, then bake in the preheated oven for 15 minutes.

Spanish Tortilla

Do pay attention to the fact that for this dish you must have a frying pan that can go under the grill. That is, not only must it fit under the grill but it must have a *heatproof* handle. If you are the proud possessor of a frying pan with a plastic handle and you try this recipe, you will end up with a rather deformed handle!

SERVES 2–3 • PREP 25 min

INGREDIENTS

3 tablespoons oil
300g potato, finely cubed
knob of butter
1 onion, diced
2 cloves garlic, crushed
1 red pepper, diced
4 eggs, beaten
pinch of oregano
salt and pepper

METHOD

1 Heat the oil in a frying pan and fry the potato until it has cooked and browned (about 6–8 minutes).

2 Remove the potato from the pan, add the butter and fry the onion, garlic and pepper for 5 minutes. Return the potato to the pan and pour in the eggs, which will quickly begin to set. Sprinkle with oregano and season.

3 Cook on a low heat for 2 minutes.

4 Preheat the grill.

5 Put the frying pan under the grill and cook until the top of the tortilla is golden brown. Slide on to a plate and cut into wedges.

6 Serve with crusty bread and salad – or, not authentically, with baked beans and grilled tomatoes.

Cheese Boreks

Some make a big fuss about using filo pastry but I find it very easy to use and don't bother with damp tea towels, etc. Just don't go walkabout in the middle of making these because the pastry will become crisp and unusable if left too long.

SERVES 4 • PREP 10 min • COOKING 15 min

INGREDIENTS

100g feta cheese, crumbled
1 egg, beaten
1 tablespoon fresh chopped mint
4 sheets filo pastry
25g melted butter

METHOD

1 Preheat the oven to 180°C/350°F/Gas 4.

2 Mix together the cheese, egg and mint.

3 Cut each sheet of filo pastry into 3 equal lengths and brush with the melted butter.

4 Place a large teaspoon of mixture at one side of each strip of pastry, roll the pastry over the filling twice, then fold the ends in and continue rolling, so that you have a neat cigar shape with the filling completely enclosed.

5 Put on a greased baking tray and brush with butter.

6 Repeat until you have 12 boreks.

7 Bake in the preheated oven for about 15 minutes until crisp and golden. Serve with a lemony green salad.

Mushrooms *à la Grecque*

SERVES 4 • PREP 15 min

INGREDIENTS

8 tablespoons olive oil
2 large onions, sliced
2 cloves garlic, crushed
600g economy mushrooms,
  cleaned and any tough
  stalks removed
8 tomatoes, cut into wedges
100g stoned black olives
2 tablespoons (30ml)
  white wine vinegar
salt and black pepper

METHOD

1 Heat 2 tablespoons of the oil and gently fry the onions
  and garlic until they are soft and starting to brown.

2 Add the mushrooms and tomatoes and gently stir-fry
  until they are just softening.

3 Place in a serving dish and garnish with the olives.

4 Mix the rest of the oil with the vinegar, season and
  drizzle over the salad. Serve with crusty bread to mop
  up the juices.

Vegetables in Creamy Mustard Sauce with Chorizo

SERVES 2 • PREP 30 min

INGREDIENTS

2 tablespoons oil
1 onion, chopped
225g potatoes, peeled and thinly sliced
2 carrots, peeled and thinly sliced
300ml vegetable stock, made
    with 1 stock cube and boiling water
150ml carton single cream
1 heaped tablespoon wholegrain mustard
50g chorizo sausage, salami type,
    thinly sliced
salt and black pepper

METHOD

1 Heat the oil in a pan and fry the onion and potatoes for a few minutes until they soften and start to brown.

2 Add the carrots and stock, cover tightly and simmer for 20 minutes until the vegetables are cooked.

3 Just before serving, stir in the other ingredients, season, warm through and serve.

TIP   Serve with rice.
Other cooked sausages can be substituted for the chorizo.

Tomato, Leek and Bacon Rice

SERVES 4 • PREP 30 min

INGREDIENTS

2 tablespoons oil
2 large leeks, sliced
1 clove garlic, crushed
125g bacon, chopped
400g can chopped tomatoes
250g long-grain rice
700ml chicken stock, made with
  1 stock cube and boiling water
black pepper

METHOD

1 Heat the oil in a pan and fry the leeks, garlic and bacon for a few minutes until they soften and start to brown.

2 Add the tomatoes and rice and cook for 1 minute.

3 Add the stock, season with black pepper and simmer until the rice is cooked and the stock has been absorbed.

4 Stir and serve immediately.

Veggieburgers

SERVES 4 • PREP 25 min

INGREDIENTS

4 vegetarian burgers
4 sesame seed burger buns
3 tablespoons chilli relish

METHOD

1 Preheat the oven to the temperature indicated on the packaging.

2 Place the burgers on a baking tray and cook in the preheated oven as directed on the packaging, turning once.

3 Split the buns in half.

4 When the burgers are cooked, put one on each bun, top with the chilli relish and cover with the remaining bun halves. Serve immediately.

PASTA DISHES

Risotto with Mushrooms and Walnuts

SERVES 2 • PREP 25 min

INGREDIENTS

1 tablespoon oil
1 onion, chopped
200g mushrooms, sliced
125g risotto rice
450ml vegetable stock
100g walnuts, broken
salt and black pepper

METHOD

1   Heat the oil in a pan and fry the onion until soft.

2   Stir in the mushrooms and rice. Gently stir-fry for 1 minute until the rice is fully covered with oil.

3   Add the stock 150ml at a time and allow this to be absorbed before adding more.

(continued over)

4 When all the stock has been absorbed, the rice should be cooked through and have a creamy consistency. (You can add more stock if you think it needs it – but don't overcook it.)

5 Stir in the walnuts, season and serve.

TIP Non-vegans can stir in a little butter just before serving. A little cream or mascarpone is also nice – but not worth buying just for this one dish.

Risi e Bisi

SERVES 4 • PREP 25 min

INGREDIENTS

1 tablespoon olive oil
1 tablespoon butter
1 onion, chopped
2 cloves garlic, crushed
250g risotto rice
900ml chicken stock, made with
  1 stock cube and boiling water
450g frozen peas
25g Parmesan cheese, grated
100g ham, finely chopped
bunch of parsley, finely chopped
salt and black pepper

METHOD

1 Heat the oil and butter in a pan and fry the onion and garlic until they start to brown.

2 Add the rice, give it a quick stir, then add 300ml of the stock.

3 Cook until that stock is absorbed, then add another 300ml of stock.

4 When that is absorbed, add the rest of the stock and the peas.

(continued over)

5 When the stock is nearly absorbed, the rice should be cooked.

6 Stir in the Parmesan, ham and parsley, season and serve immediately.

Quick Pizza

SERVES 4 • PREP 15 min • Cooking 12–15 min

INGREDIENTS

400g can chopped tomatoes
1 tablespoon tomato purée
sprinkling of oregano
2 large pizza bases
100–150g cheese
2 tablespoons sweetcorn
2 tablespoons pineapple pieces
black pepper

METHOD

1 Preheat the oven to 230°C/450°F/Gas 8.

2 Simmer the tomatoes, tomato purée and oregano for 10 minutes until you have a thick sauce.

3 Divide this between the pizza bases, coating them evenly.

4 Slice the cheese over the tomato mixture, then top with the sweetcorn and pineapple, and season with black pepper.

5 Bake in the preheated oven for 12–15 minutes.

Macaroni Cheese

SERVES 2 • PREP 25 min

INGREDIENTS

125g macaroni
1 tablespoon oil
1 onion, chopped
350ml cheese sauce
50g cheese, grated

METHOD

1 Cook the macaroni in boiling water, as directed on the packet, then drain.

2 While you are cooking the macaroni, heat the oil in a pan and fry the onion until brown.

3 Meanwhile, preheat the grill. Mix together the cheese sauce with the cooked and drained macaroni.

4 Place in a heatproof dish and cover with the cheese.

5 Grill under the preheated grill until the cheese bubbles and browns.

TIP   Serve with a green salad. You can also add sliced or halved tomatoes, cubes of cooked ham or minced chilli for a spicy version.

Chorizo and Pepper Sauce (for Pasta)

SERVES 4 • PREP 25 min

INGREDIENTS

2 tablespoons oil

1 onion, sliced

3 peppers of mixed colours,
  deseeded and sliced

2 cloves garlic, crushed

150g chorizo, salami type,
  peeled and cut into chunks

400g can chopped tomatoes

1 teaspoon dried oregano

salt and black pepper

METHOD

1 Heat the oil in a pan and fry the onion, peppers, garlic and chorizo until the vegetables are soft and starting to brown.

2 Add the tomatoes and oregano, season and cook for 10 minutes to thicken the sauce before serving.

Farfalle with Pepperoni and Olives

SERVES 4 • PREP 25 min

INGREDIENTS

400g farfalle pasta
2 tablespoons oil
2 onions, chopped
2 cloves garlic, crushed
1 teaspoon minced chilli
400g can chopped tomatoes
100g pepperoni, roughly chopped
50g stoned black olives

METHOD

1 Put the water on to boil for the pasta.

2 Heat the oil in a pan and fry the onions and garlic until they are soft and starting to brown.

3 Cook the farfalle in plenty of boiling water as directed on the packet.

4 To the browned onions, add the chilli and tomatoes, cover and simmer until the pasta is ready.

5 When the pasta is cooked, drain it and divide it among 4 serving bowls.

6 Stir the pepperoni and olives into the sauce and spoon it over the pasta.

Pasta with Sausage Sauce

SERVES 4 • PREP 30 min

INGREDIENTS

1 tablespoon oil
1 large onion, chopped
2 cloves garlic
1 teaspoon minced chilli (optional)
1 packet sausages (6 sausages)
350–500ml tomato sauce for pasta
    (home-made or from a jar)
330g pasta

METHOD

1 Heat the oil in a pan and fry the onion, garlic and chilli (if using) gently for 5 minutes.

2 Take the skins off the sausages and chop up the meat.

3 Add the meat to the pan and fry until it has browned, breaking up any lumps as you go.

4 Add the tomato sauce and simmer gently while you cook the pasta as directed on the packet.

5 Drain the pasta and serve with the sausage sauce.

Spaghetti Bolognese

SERVES 4 • PREP 25 min

INGREDIENTS

1 tablespoon oil
1 large onion, finely chopped
2 cloves garlic, crushed
500g beef mince
2 tablespoons tomato purée
1 teaspoon oregano
1 beef stock cube
400g can chopped tomatoes
150ml red wine or water
salt and pepper
330g spaghetti
grated Parmesan cheese to serve

METHOD

1   Put a large saucepan of water on to boil for the spaghetti.

2   Heat the oil in a pan and fry the onion and garlic gently for 5 minutes. Push the onions to the side of the pan and add the beef mince. Fry briskly until no signs of pink remain.

3   Add the tomato purée and oregano and mix well. Sprinkle in the beef cube, then add the tomatoes and red wine or water. Season.

4   Stir thoroughly and let the sauce simmer gently while you cook the spaghetti.

5   Put the spaghetti in the boiling water and cook as directed on the packet. Drain the cooked spaghetti and serve with the Bolognese sauce and freshly grated Parmesan.

PASTA AL FORNO (BAKED PASTA)

Use the meat sauce from this recipe and mix it with 330g of any cooked pasta. Place in an ovenproof dish and cover with 350ml cheese sauce and a sprinkling of cheese. Cook in a preheated oven or under a grill until the cheese is bubbling and browning. It is just as nice as lasagne but even quicker to make.

Veggie Spag Bol

A perennial favourite when entertaining a friend: what can be nicer than a bowl of spaghetti and a glass of wine? We love garlic bread with this dish (although a salad would be a healthier alternative). Why not compromise and serve a salad *and* garlic bread!

SERVES 2 • PREP 30 min

INGREDIENTS

50g split red lentils
2 tablespoons oil
1 onion, sliced
1 clove garlic, crushed
100g mushrooms, chopped
200g can chopped tomatoes
1 tablespoon tomato purée
sprinkling of oregano
150g spaghetti

METHOD

1 Cook the lentils in boiling water for 10 minutes. Drain.

2 Heat the oil in a pan and fry the onion, garlic and mushrooms for 10 minutes until they are soft.

3 Add to the lentils with the tomatoes, tomato purée and oregano.

4 Simmer gently for 5–10 minutes.

5 Meanwhile, cook the spaghetti in boiling water as directed on the packet. When it is ready, drain it and serve it with the lentil mixture.

Pasta with Roasted Veg

SERVES 4 • PREP 30 min

INGREDIENTS

800g mixed vegetables,
   including red pepper, onion,
   courgettes, mushrooms, tomatoes
1 clove garlic, crushed
sprinkling of dried thyme
olive oil
350g pasta – bows or
   spirals are very good

METHOD

1 Preheat the oven to its highest temperature.

2 Slice, halve or roughly dice the vegetables.

3 Put them in a bowl with the garlic and thyme and use
   just enough oil to coat them all.

4 Transfer the vegetables to a roasting sheet and cook,
   uncovered, in the preheated oven for 15–20 minutes
   until they are soft and blackening at the edges.

5 Cook the pasta as directed on the packet.

6 Drain the pasta and serve topped with the roasted
   vegetables.

STIR-FRIES AND CURRIES

Thai Prawn Curry

SERVES 4 • PREP 25 min

INGREDIENTS

1 tablespoon oil
1 onion, chopped
1 clove garlic, crushed
1 teaspoon minced ginger
1 tablespoon Thai red curry paste
400g can coconut milk
450g frozen large, uncooked prawns

METHOD

1 Heat the oil in a pan and fry the onion, garlic and ginger until the onion is softened and starting to brown.

2 Blend in the curry paste with a little of the coconut milk, then add the rest of the coconut milk.

3 Cook, uncovered, until the sauce has reduced and thickened a little.

4 Add the prawns and cook for a few minutes until they have cooked through (they change colour). Serve immediately.

Teriyaki Chicken Stir-fry

SERVES 4 • PREP 20 min + MARINADING TIME

INGREDIENTS

*2 medium boneless, skinless chicken breasts,
  cut into thin strips*

2 tablespoons soy sauce

1 tablespoon oil

*2 large carrots, peeled and cut
  into small matchsticks*

*1 red pepper, deseeded and cut into
  small matchsticks*

*1 green pepper, deseeded and cut into
  small matchsticks*

150g jar Teriyaki stir-fry sauce

bunch of spring onions, chopped

METHOD

1 Marinate the chicken in the soy sauce for 10 minutes, or
   longer if possible.

2 Heat the oil in a frying pan and fry the chicken and
   marinate for 2 minutes.

3 Add the carrots and both peppers and stir-fry for 4
   minutes.

4 Add the sauce and spring onions and warm through.

TIP   Serve with plain boiled rice or boiled noodles.

Vegetable Curry (microwave)

SERVES 4 • PREP 20 min + STANDING TIME

INGREDIENTS

2 tablespoons oil

1 teaspoon black mustard seeds

1 teaspoon cumin seeds

1 teaspoon coriander

1 teaspoon turmeric

1 onion, thinly sliced

2 cloves garlic, crushed

1 teaspoon minced ginger

250g mixed vegetables, such as carrots, courgettes, cauliflower, green beans, mushrooms and peas, cut into bite-sized pieces (hard vegetables should be cut into smaller pieces)

400g can chopped tomatoes

1 heaped tablespoon sultanas

salt and pepper

garam masala for sprinkling

METHOD

1 Put the oil and spices in a microwaveable bowl.

2 Cover and cook for 1 minute.

(continued over)

3 Add the onion, garlic and ginger, and mix well.

4 Cook for 2 minutes.

5 Add the mixed vegetables, and cook for 5 minutes.

6 Add the tomatoes and sultanas, season and mix well. Cook for 3 minutes.

7 Let it stand for 5 minutes. Sprinkle with garam masala and stir.

TIP For a creamier curry, you can mix in a tablespoon or 2 of cream, crème fraîche or yogurt just before serving.

Coconut Chicken Curry

SERVES 2 • PREP 30 min

INGREDIENTS

1 tablespoon oil
1 onion, diced
½ green pepper, deseeded and diced
350g chicken thighs, boned and skinned
100g mushrooms, quartered
2 tablespoons korma curry paste
1 teaspoon minced lemongrass (optional)
1 teaspoon minced ginger
2 cloves garlic, crushed
1 tablespoon soy sauce
200ml carton coconut cream
handful of basil leaves (optional)

METHOD

1 Heat the oil in a pan and fry the onion and pepper for 5 minutes until they start to brown.

2 Add the chicken thighs and fry for another 5 minutes.

3 Add the mushrooms, curry paste, lemongrass (if using), ginger, garlic and soy sauce, and stir-fry for 2–3 minutes.

4 Add the coconut cream, stir well, cover and simmer for 5 minutes.

5 Stir in the basil (if using) just before serving.

TIP   Serve with rice and a side salad of tomatoes and onion.

Vegetable Biryani

SERVES 4 • PREP 25 min

INGREDIENTS

6 cardamom pods, lightly crushed

1 tablespoon coriander

1 teaspoon turmeric

1 teaspoon chilli powder

2.5cm piece of fresh ginger,
  cut into matchsticks

4 cloves garlic, crushed

3 tablespoons oil

100g frozen peas

320g mixed quick cook vegetables,
  e.g. courgettes, peppers, beans,
  mushrooms, sliced

250g basmati rice

1 large onion, chopped

1 tablespoon korma curry paste

150ml double cream

2 heaped tablespoons sultanas

1 tablespoon toasted almonds

METHOD

1 Using a large saucepan, stir-fry the spices, ginger and half the garlic in 2 tablespoons of the oil for 1 minute.

2 Add the vegetables and stir-fry for 2 minutes.

3 Add the rice and stir-fry for another minute before covering everything with water.

4 Bring to the boil, cover, reduce the heat and cook for 10 minutes until the rice and vegetables are tender and the water is absorbed.

5 Meanwhile, gently fry the onion and korma curry paste in the remaining oil for 5 minutes.

6 Add the cream and simmer gently until the rice and vegetables are cooked.

7 Mix the rice and vegetables with the sultanas and toasted almonds.

8 Serve with the curry sauce on top.

Saag Aloo (Spinach and Potato Curry)

SERVES 2 AS A MAIN DISH OR 4 AS AN ACCOMPANIMENT
• PREPARATION 30 min

INGREDIENTS

3 tablespoons oil

4 medium potatoes (about 500g),
  peeled and cut into 2–3 cm chunks

½ teaspoon turmeric

½ teaspoon cumin or, in place of these,
1 tablespoon mild curry powder

½ teaspoon black pepper

½ teaspoon mild chilli powder

1 large onion, chopped

2 cloves garlic, crushed

225g bag baby spinach

3–4 tomatoes (about 160g),
  seeds removed and flesh chopped

salt

METHOD

1 In a frying pan with a lid, heat 2 tablespoons of the oil.

2 Add the potatoes and spices and mix well so that potatoes are coated with the oil.

3 Put the lid on the pan, reduce the heat and cook for 8 minutes, stirring occasionally to prevent sticking.

4 Remove the potatoes from the pan and heat the remaining tablespoon of oil, add the onion and garlic and gently cook for 5 minutes.

5 Add the spinach in two batches, putting the second batch in when the first has wilted down.

6 Lastly, add the tomatoes, the cooked potatoes and season with salt.

7 Cover and cook gently for 5 minutes.

MEAT DISHES

Baked Lemon Chicken

SERVES 2 • PREP 5 min • COOKING 25 min

INGREDIENTS

4–6 chicken thighs, boned and skinned
1 tablespoon oil
juice of ½ lemon
1 tablespoon soy sauce
1 teaspoon sugar

METHOD

1 Preheat the oven to 190°C/375°F/Gas 5.

2 Put the chicken thighs in a single layer in an ovenproof dish.

3 Spoon over the oil, lemon juice and soy sauce.

4 Sprinkle with the sugar.

5 Cook in the preheated oven for 25 minutes.

6 Serve hot or cold.

TIP   Serve hot with rice or cold with salad.

Chicken and Banana Creole

SERVES 2 • PREP 30 min

INGREDIENTS

125g long-grain rice
330ml chicken stock, made with
  1 stock cube and boiling water
2 tablespoons oil
1 medium chicken breast,
  boned and skinned, cut into strips
1 onion, chopped
1 clove garlic, crushed
½ green pepper, thickly sliced
400g can red kidney beans,
  drained and rinsed
1 teaspoon minced chilli
1 banana, thickly sliced

METHOD

1 Place the rice in a pan with a tightly fitting lid and cook gently in the stock until all the stock has been absorbed.

2 Meanwhile, heat the oil and gently fry the chicken, onion, garlic and pepper until they are soft and starting to brown.

3 Add the beans, cover and cook until heated through.

4 Add the remaining ingredients, mix together well and serve on the cooked rice.

Sausages with Onion Gravy

SERVES 4 • PREP 30 min

INGREDIENTS

2 tablespoons oil

12 sausages

2 large onions, sliced

2 teaspoons sugar

1 tablespoon wholegrain
  mustard (optional)

dash of Worcestershire sauce

300ml gravy, made up with
  6 heaped teaspoons gravy
  granules

METHOD

1 Preheat the oven to 200°C/400°F/Gas 6.

2 Put half the oil in a roasting pan and put the pan in the oven to heat the oil. After 5 minutes, put the sausages in the roasting tin and toss to make sure everything is covered in oil. Return to the oven for 10 minutes.

3 Put the other tablespoon of oil in a frying pan and cook the onions for 5–10 minutes until they are browning.

4 Turn the sausages over and cook for another 10 minutes or until they are cooked through.

5 Stir the sugar into the onions and then the rest of ingredients. Simmer gently for 10 minutes.

6 When the sausages are cooked, serve with the onion gravy.

Chicken Nachos

SERVES 4 • PREP 25 min

INGREDIENTS

4 chicken breasts (about 125–150g each),
  boned and skinned
oil for brushing
140g bag nachos
300g jar salsa
150ml sour cream
200g Cheddar cheese, grated

METHOD

1 Preheat the oven to 200°C/400°F/Gas 6.

2 Make 3 deep slashes in each chicken breast and then spread them out on a baking tray.

3 Brush with a little oil and then bake in the preheated oven for 15 minutes. Check that the chicken is cooked. (No pink juices should appear when the meat is pierced.)

4 Top each chicken breast with salsa and then sour cream. Spread the nachos over the dish and then cover with grated cheese.

5 Cook in the oven for a few minutes until the cheese is melting. Serve immediately.

Tortilla-topped Mexican Pie

SERVES 4 • PREP 30 min

INGREDIENTS

FOR THE FILLING

2 tablespoons oil

1 large onion, chopped

2 cloves garlic, crushed

2 carrots, diced

500g minced beef

1–3 teaspoons chilli powder, to taste

1 teaspoon cumin

1 beef stock cube

1 teaspoon oregano

400g can red kidney beans,
   drained and rinsed

FOR THE TOPPING

40g packet tortilla chips

150ml sour cream

100g cheese, grated

METHOD

1 Preheat the oven to 180°C/350°F/Gas 4.

2 Heat the oil in a pan and fry the onion, garlic and
   carrots until they have softened.

3 Add the beef and chilli powder, and cook for a further
   5 minutes to brown the meat.

(continued over)

4 Add the rest of the ingredients, mix well and place in an ovenproof dish.

5 Cover with the tortillas and sour cream and sprinkle with the cheese.

6 Bake in the preheated oven for 10–15 minutes, until the cheese is melting.

Chilli con Carne

SERVES 4 • PREP 10 min • COOKING 20 min

INGREDIENTS

1 tablespoon oil

1 large onion, chopped

2 cloves garlic, crushed

1–3 teaspoons chilli powder, to taste

1 teaspoon cumin

500g minced beef

1 beef stock cube

1 teaspoon oregano

2 tablespoons tomato purée

2 teaspoons soft brown sugar
  or 2 pieces dark chocolate

400g can chopped tomatoes

250ml hot water

400g can kidney beans,
  rinsed and drained

salt and pepper

METHOD

1 Heat the oil in a large frying pan with a lid.

2 Cook the onion for 5 minutes until it starts to soften.

3 Add the garlic, chilli powder and cumin and stir-fry for 30 seconds. Push the onions to the side of the pan and add the beef. Quickly stir-fry until no signs of pink remain.

(continued over)

4 Crumble in the stock cube, add the oregano and tomato purée and stir well before adding the sugar or chocolate.

5 Add the tomatoes and water.

6 Cover and cook gently for 15 minutes.

7 Add the beans and season to taste. Simmer for 5 minutes just to warm the beans through.

Chicken Fajitas

SERVES 4 • PREP 25 min

INGREDIENTS

2 tablespoons oil

450g chicken (about 3 chicken breasts),
  cut into slices

1 red onion, sliced

1 red pepper, diced

1 green pepper, diced

2 tomatoes, skinned (page 221)
  and chopped

2 cloves garlic, crushed

sprinkling of chilli powder

pinch of ground coriander

8 tortillas

METHOD

1 Heat the oil and stir-fry the chicken until it browns. Add
   the onion and peppers and fry for 5 minutes.

2 Then add the tomatoes, garlic, chilli and coriander and
   fry for a further 5 minutes.

3 Use as a stuffing for the tortillas.

TIP   Fajitas are usually served with salad, grated cheese, sour cream
         and salsa.

---

4 More Time to Cook
food to share, including roasts for Sundays

Here are some dishes for when you've got a little time to spare and want to indulge yourself, or for friends who want to cook together. There are Sunday roasts and some alternatives – it's easy to produce a baked dish that can be served with some simple veg or a salad. A Sunday lunch is often the occasion that brings people together to cook for the first time, but it does need a little organisation. You must decide how many you are cooking for, what the menu is going to be, make out your shopping list, do the shopping, the cooking and, last but not least, the washing up! Once it is decided who will do what, this is much easier to organise than it sounds. Another option is that each person is totally responsible for one dish. But if you are doing it this way, you still need to make sure that everyone knows how much they have spent, so that you can add up the expenses and divide the total among you, to ensure that the person doing the main dish doesn't bear the brunt of the cost. I know some people prefer this second method, but it can run into more problems . . . If someone doesn't get up in time, for instance, you may find yourself without some of your lunch!

Still, it is one of the pleasures of life to be able to sit down with some friends and a bottle or two and really pig out. The afternoon should be kept free as the stupor produced by these meals usually entails a siesta!

I remember one afternoon when some of us had booked a court to play badminton . . . What a waste of money! When the time came, nobody wanted to go and we couldn't bring ourselves to run about the court. We all stood about moaning 'yours' as the shuttlecock passed us by. A big mistake! We now play badminton on Sunday morning – proving that old age can bring wisdom.

THE CHOICES:

SOUPS

French Onion Soup

Cheese and Vegetable Soup

Baked Bean, Pancetta and Vegetable Soup

Minestrone

Pistou

Bean and Tomato Soup

EASY SNACKS

Jacket Potatoes Filled with Avocado and Bacon

Shortcrust Pastry

Broccoli, Cheese and Tomato Quiche

Mushroom Quiche

Ratatouille

Oven-baked Ratatouille

Ratatouille-filled Lasagne Rolls

Undercover Beans Cheese 'n' Lentil Bake

Mexican Vegetarian Chilli Casserole

Veggie Winter Warmer

Vegetarian Pasta Bake

Vegetable Korma

Vegetarian Goulash (By-election Slops)

Vegetarian Cassoulet

Sue's Vegetarian Chilli

Imam Bayildi (The Priest Fainted)

Winter Warmer

PIZZA AND PASTA

Pizza Dough

Tomato Sauce (for Pizza and Pasta)

Pizza with Peppers and Mushrooms

Pizza Casa

Tomato and Aubergine Sauce (for Pasta)

Pasta Primavera

Roman Gnocchi (Semolina)

CHICKEN DISHES

Chicken Enchiladas

Chicken Burritos

Chicken Korma

Tandoori Chicken

West Country Chicken

X-tra Nice Chicken

Pot-roasted Chicken

Italian Garlic Chicken Casserole

Chicken and Chick Pea Stew

Jambalaya

Moroccan Lemon Chicken with Olives

BEEF DISHES

Mince Bake with Cheesy Pasta Topping

Lasagne

Mince, Baked Bean and Potato Pie

Bobotie

Beef Stew

ROASTS

Stuffed Nut Roast

Roast Chicken

Roast Pork

Roast Lamb

Roast Beef

SOUPS

French Onion Soup

This makes a great meal for two, served with garlic bread and red wine.

SERVES 2 • PREP 20 min • COOKING 20 min

INGREDIENTS

75g butter
4 onions, sliced thinly
1 tablespoon plain flour
1 clove garlic, crushed
2 onion stock cubes
750ml boiling water
salt and pepper
4 slices French bread
50g cheese, grated

METHOD

1 Melt the butter in a pan and fry the onions for 10 minutes until they are soft and browning.

2 Stir in the flour and garlic, mixing well.

3 Dissolve the stock cubes in the water, add this to the onion mixture and season.

4 Bring to the boil, then simmer for 20 minutes.

5 Preheat the grill.

6 Put the bread on the grill tray, sprinkle with the cheese and grill until the cheese starts to melt.

7 Ladle the soup into bowls and float two slices of bread in each one.

Cheese and Vegetable Soup

SERVES 2 • PREP 25 min • COOKING 20 min

INGREDIENTS

1 tablespoon olive oil
1 onion, chopped
1 medium potato, peeled and diced
250g carrots (about 3 carrots, depending on size)
500ml vegetable stock
100g Cheddar cheese, grated
dash of Worcestershire sauce (optional)
salt and pepper

METHOD

1 Heat the oil in a pan and fry the onion gently for 5 minutes.

2 Add the potato and carrots and stir.

3 Cover and reduce the heat. Cook for 10 minutes, stirring occasionally.

4 Add the stock and simmer for 20 minutes.

5 Stir in the cheese, add the Worcestershire sauce (if using) and continue to cook until the cheese melts.

6 Season and serve.

Baked Bean, Pancetta and Vegetable Soup

SERVES 2 • PREP 15 min • COOKING 25 min

INGREDIENTS

1 tablespoon olive oil
1 onion, chopped
85g cubes of pancetta
1 large carrot, chopped
1 medium potato, peeled and diced
250ml passata (sieved tomatoes)
500ml vegetable stock
200g can baked beans
salt and pepper

METHOD

1 Heat the oil in a medium pan and cook the onion and pancetta for 5 minutes.

2 Add the carrot and potato and cook for 2–3 minutes.

3 Add the passata and stock, bring to the boil, cover and reduce the heat.

4 Simmer gently for 25 minutes.

5 Add the beans, stir well and continue to cook until the beans are warmed through.

6 Season and serve.

TIP You can vary the soup by adding curried or barbecued beans.

Minestrone

SERVES 4 • PREP 35 min + SOAKING TIME • COOKING 30 min

INGREDIENTS

200g dried borlotti beans
2 tablespoons olive oil
1 large onion, chopped
1 clove garlic, crushed
2 carrots, halved, then sliced
2 medium potatoes, peeled and diced
500ml passata
100g frozen peas or broad beans
100g small pasta for soup
salt and pepper
Parmesan cheese, freshly grated, to serve

METHOD

1 Start this the night before you want to eat by putting the borlotti beans in a large bowl, covering them with cold water and leaving them to soak.

2 When you are ready to start cooking, drain the beans and rinse well.

3 Put the beans in a medium saucepan and cover them with water.

4 Bring to the boil, then cover and simmer very gently for about an hour or until the beans are tender.

5 When the beans have been cooking for 30 minutes, put the oil in a large saucepan and gently fry the onion, garlic, carrots and potatoes for 10 minutes.

6 Add the passata and simmer gently until the beans are ready.

7 Drain the beans, add them to the soup with the peas or broad beans and pasta, season and continue to cook until the pasta is tender.

8 Serve with grated Parmesan.

Pistou

SERVES 2–4 • PREP 40 min

INGREDIENTS

2 tablespoons olive oil
1 onion, chopped
1 clove garlic, crushed
200g carrots, diced
1 green or red pepper, diced
400g can chopped tomatoes
250ml vegetable stock
50g small pasta shapes
1–2 tablespoons pesto

METHOD

1 Heat the oil in a pan and cook the onion, garlic, carrots and pepper until they are soft.

2 Add the tomatoes and stock and bring to the boil.

3 Cover and simmer for 15 minutes.

4 Add the pasta shapes and cook for a further 10 minutes.

5 Stir in the pesto and serve with crusty French bread.

Bean and Tomato Soup

SERVES 2–3 • PREP 15 min + SOAKING TIME • COOKING 45–55 min

INGREDIENTS

1 tablespoon oil
1 onion, chopped
2 large cloves garlic, peeled and left whole
100g dried borlotti beans, soaked for at least 12 hours
knob of butter
350ml water
1 bay leaf (optional)
pinch of mixed herbs, dried thyme or oregano
2 teaspoons wholegrain mustard
1 tablespoon tomato purée
300ml tomato juice

METHOD

1 Heat the oil in a large pan and fry the onion and garlic for 5 minutes.

2 Add the drained beans and butter and stir-fry for 1–2 minutes.

3 Add the water, the bay leaf (if using) and the herbs.

4 Bring to the boil, then cover and simmer as gently as possible for 45–55 minutes, until the beans are tender.

5 Remove the bay leaf (if using) and mash the garlic into the beans.

6 Add the rest of ingredients and simmer gently for 5 minutes.

EASY SNACKS

Jacket Potatoes Filled with Avocado and Bacon

SERVES 4 • PREP 5 min • COOKING 60–90 min

INGREDIENTS

4 large potatoes

FOR THE FILLING
4 rashers bacon, grilled until crispy
1 avocado, peeled, stoned and cubed
salt and black pepper

METHOD

1 Preheat the oven to 220°C/425°F/Gas 7.

2 Prick the potatoes all over with a fork and cook in the preheated oven for 1–1½ hours until they are crispy outside and soft and fluffy inside.

3 Meanwhile, prepare your filling.

4 Crumble or dice the bacon, mix with the avocado, and season.

5 Cut a large cross in the top of each potato and squeeze gently to open it out, then top with the filling.

Shortcrust Pastry

Although you can buy pastry either frozen or chilled, here are some recipes that you may want to try. Don't worry if you have trouble rolling out your pastry – you can simply press it into your dish to fit.

MAKES ABOUT 325g • PREP 10 MINUTES + RESTING TIME

INGREDIENTS

200g flour
pinch of salt
125g butter
cold water

METHOD

1 Put the flour, salt and butter into a bowl.

2 Rub the mixture between your fingertips until it resembles fine breadcrumbs.

3 Add a few tablespoons of water – only as much as you need to form a dough.

4 Wrap the dough in clingfilm and rest it in the fridge for 20 minutes before using it.

5 Roll out the dough on a floured surface with a rolling pin, handling it as little as possible.

(continued over)

TIP Baking 'blind' helps to produce a crispy pastry shell for quiches. Preheat the oven to 190°C/375°F/Gas 5. Line a 20cm flan tin with the pastry, then prick the base of the pastry all over with a fork. Put some greaseproof paper in the bottom and weigh it down with some coins. Bake in the preheated oven for 15 minutes. Remove the paper and coins before using the pastry shell.

CHEESE PASTRY

Add 75g grated cheese, a pinch of dried mustard powder and an egg yolk to the 'breadcrumb' mixture.

NUTTY PASTRY

Add 50g roasted chopped hazelnuts and an egg yolk to the 'breadcrumb' mixture.

Broccoli, Cheese and Tomato Quiche

To skin tomatoes, put them in a bowl, cover them with boiling water and leave them until the skin can be peeled away easily. Be careful when taking the tomatoes out, as the water will still be very hot!

SERVES 3–4 • PREP 10 min • COOKING 35–45 min

INGREDIENTS

400g Cheese Pastry (page 220)

150g broccoli florets, cooked

2 plum tomatoes, skinned and
  cut into wedges

75g cheese, grated

2 eggs, beaten

125ml carton single cream

salt and pepper

chopped fresh herbs, such as chives
  (optional)

METHOD

1 Preheat the oven to 190°C/375°F/Gas 5.

2 Bake the pastry blind (page 220). Fill with the broccoli, tomatoes and half the cheese.

3 Mix together the eggs and cream, season well, and add the herbs (if using).

(continued over)

4 Pour the egg mixture into the pastry case.

5 Sprinkle with the remaining cheese and bake in the oven for 35–45 minutes.

TIP You can substitute baby cherry tomatoes for the plum tomatoes; use 10–12 and cut in half (they don't need skinning).

Mushroom Quiche

SERVES 3–4 • PREP 10 min • COOKING 35–45 min

INGREDIENTS

375g Nutty Pastry (page 220)
small knob of butter
200g mushrooms, sliced
75g cheese, grated
chopped fresh herbs, such as chives
  (optional)
2 eggs, beaten
150ml carton single cream
salt and pepper

METHOD

1 Preheat the oven to 190°C/375°F/Gas 5.

2 Bake the pastry blind (page 220).

3 Melt the butter in a pan and fry the mushrooms gently for 1–2 minutes.

4 Put them in the pastry case with half the cheese and the herbs (if using).

5 Beat together the eggs and cream, season and pour the mixture into the pastry case.

6 Sprinkle with the remaining cheese and bake in the preheated oven for 35–45 minutes.

Ratatouille

SERVES 4 • PREP 15 mins • COOKING 25 min

INGREDIENTS

3 tablespoons oil
1 onion, chopped
2 cloves garlic, chopped
1 red pepper, chopped
2 courgettes, chopped
1 aubergine, chopped
400g can chopped tomatoes with basil
black pepper

METHOD

1 Heat the oil in a pan and fry the onion, garlic and pepper for 5 minutes.

2 Add the courgettes and aubergine and cook for a further 5 minutes.

3 Pour in the tomatoes and season with black pepper.

4 Cover and simmer gently for 20 minutes. This dish can be served hot or cold.

Oven-baked Ratatouille

I think ratatouille is best served just warm but it can also be served cold as a salad. I have found that this makes a great filling for lasagne as well (page 271).

SERVES 4 • PREP 15 mins • COOKING 30–40 min

INGREDIENTS

200g courgette, sliced
200g aubergine, diced
1 orange pepper, diced
1 yellow pepper, diced
1 red onion, sliced
4 tomatoes, cut into wedges
4 tablespoons oil
salt and pepper

METHOD

1 Preheat the oven to 220°C/425°F/Gas 7.

2 Mix everything together, making sure that the vegetables are well coated with oil.

3 Spread the vegetables over a roasting or baking tray, season and bake in the preheated oven for 30–40 minutes or until the vegetables are starting to crisp at the edges.

4 Serve warm or cold with rice or pasta.

Ratatouille-filled Lasagne Rolls

SERVES 4–6 • PREP 10 min • COOKING 30 min

INGREDIENTS

12 sheets fresh lasagne
Oven-baked Ratatouille (page 225),
  the whole quantity
350ml Cheese Sauce (page 337)
75g cheese, grated

METHOD

1 Preheat the oven to 180°C/350°F/Gas 4.

2 Soak the lasagne sheets in boiling water for 5 minutes, then drain.

3 Lay out the pasta and divide the ratatouille between the sheets, spreading it evenly over them.

4 Roll the pasta around the ratatouille and place the rolls in a lasagne or casserole dish.

5 Cover with the cheese sauce and sprinkle with the grated cheese.

6 Bake in the preheated oven for 30 minutes.

Undercover Beans

Tortilla chips make a great topping for casseroles and we are using them more and more. It doesn't matter what size packet you get, you can use the rest for nibbles before dinner.

SERVES 4 • PREP 15 min • COOKING 45–55 min

INGREDIENTS

3 tablespoons oil
1 onion, chopped
2 cloves garlic, crushed
100g mushrooms, sliced
200g aubergine, diced
400g can chopped tomatoes
2 x 440g cans beans in chilli sauce
1 packet tortilla chips
150ml carton sour cream
75g cheese, grated

METHOD

1 Preheat the oven to 180°C/350°F/Gas 4.

2 Heat the oil in a pan and fry the onion, garlic and mushrooms for 2–3 minutes. Add the aubergine and continue to fry for 5 minutes.

3 Transfer the vegetables to a casserole dish and add the tomatoes and beans in chilli sauce. Cover and cook in the preheated oven for 45 minutes.

(continued over)

4 Remove from the oven. Spread a layer of tortilla chips over the surface of the mixture, spoon the sour cream on top and sprinkle with the cheese.

5 Return the casserole dish to the oven and continue cooking, uncovered, until the cheese is melted and bubbling.

Tip   The supermarkets' value/basics brand of tortilla chips are very useful for this recipe, and of course, incredibly cheap.

Cheese 'n' Lentil Bake

SERVES 3–4 • PREP 25 min • COOKING 50–60 min + COOLING TIME

INGREDIENTS

200g split red lentils
375ml vegetable stock or
  boiling water with 1 teaspoon Marmite
knob of butter
1 onion, diced
100g cheese, grated
salt and pepper

METHOD

1 Preheat the oven to 190°C/375°F/Gas 5.

2 Cook the lentils in the stock or boiling water until tender (15–20 minutes), adding more water if needed. You want to end up with a thick purée.

3 Meanwhile, melt the butter in a pan and cook the onion until it starts to colour.

4 When the lentils are cooked, mash with the grated cheese and onion. Season.

5 Place in a greased, 1kg loaf tin, lined with greaseproof paper.

6 Cook in the preheated oven for 50–60 minutes. Allow it to cool in the tin for 5–10 minutes and then serve.

(continued over)

LENTIL AND COURGETTE BAKE

Add 1 large grated courgette to the lentil mixture before baking.

TOMATO AND CHEESE-TOPPED BAKE

Instead of cooking the mixture in a loaf tin, put it in a lasagne or casserole dish and top with slices of tomato and more grated cheese. Bake for 40–50 minutes.

PARSLEY AND LENTIL BAKE

Add 1 tablespoon crème fraîche, a squeeze of lemon juice and 1 tablespoon chopped fresh parsley to the lentil mixture before baking.

Mexican Vegetarian Chilli Casserole

SERVES 4 • PREP 15 min • COOKING 60–70 min

INGREDIENTS

2 tablespoons oil
1 onion, chopped
1 red pepper, diced
1 green pepper, diced
450g VegeMince or Quorn
400g can chopped tomatoes
400g can beans in chilli sauce
150ml carton sour cream
tortilla chips
125g mozzarella cheese, grated

METHOD

1 Preheat the oven to 180°C/350°F/Gas 4.

2 Heat the oil in a pan and fry the onion and peppers for 5 minutes.

3 Add the VegeMince or Quorn and cook for a few minutes.

4 Stir in the tomatoes and beans and pour the mixture into a large casserole dish.

5 Cover and cook in the preheated oven for 1 hour.

6 Remove from the oven and top with the sour cream. Cover the surface with tortilla chips, then sprinkle with the cheese.

7 Return to the oven and cook, uncovered, until the cheese melts.

Veggie Winter Warmer

SERVES 4–6 • PREP 20 min • COOKING 50 min

INGREDIENTS

700g potatoes, thickly sliced

2 tablespoons oil

2 onions, chopped

*560g veggie sausages, defrosted
  if frozen and cut into chunks*

2 x 400g cans chilli beans

*200ml vegetable stock, made with
  1 stock cube and boiling water*

1 tablespoon wholegrain mustard

50g butter

salt and black pepper

METHOD

1 Preheat the oven to 190°C/375°F/Gas 5.

2 Boil the potatoes for 5 minutes, then drain well.

3 Meanwhile, heat the oil in a pan and fry the onions and sausages until they are starting to brown.

4 Mix together the onions, sausages, chilli beans and stock and place in a shallow ovenproof dish.

5 Cover with the potatoes.

6 Mix together the mustard and butter and spoon the mixture over the potatoes.

7 Season, then bake, uncovered, in the preheated oven for 50 minutes.

Vegetarian Pasta Bake

SERVES 4–6 • PREP 30 min • COOKING 25 min

INGREDIENTS

4 tablespoons oil

1 onion, chopped

3 peppers of mixed colours,
  deseeded and cubed

2 courgettes, halved and sliced

250g mushrooms, sliced

400g can chopped tomatoes

1 tablespoon tomato purée

4 sun-dried tomatoes, sliced

1 teaspoon dried oregano

salt and pepper

300g penne pasta

350ml cheese sauce,
  home made or bought

50g Cheddar cheese, grated

METHOD

1 Preheat the oven to 190°C/375°F/Gas 5.

2 Heat the oil in a pan and fry the onion for about 5
   minutes until it starts to brown.

3 Add the peppers, courgettes and mushrooms and fry for
   another 10 minutes. Add the tomatoes, tomato purée,
   sun-dried tomatoes and oregano. Season and simmer
   for 10 minutes.

(continued over)

4 Meanwhile, cook the pasta in boiling water as directed on the packet, then drain and mix with the cheese sauce.

5 Put the cooked vegetables in a large ovenproof dish and top with the cheesy pasta. Sprinkle with the grated cheese and bake in the preheated oven for 25 minutes until golden brown on top.

Vegetable Korma

SERVES 2–4 • PREP 15 min • COOKING 25 min

INGREDIENTS

2 tablespoons oil
2 tablespoons korma paste
1 large onion, diced
2 cloves garlic, crushed
2 medium potatoes (about 150g each),
   peeled and cut into 2.5cm chunks
200g butternut squash,
   peeled and cut into 2.5cm chunks
100g frozen peas
400ml coconut milk
1 tablespoon ground almonds

METHOD

1 Heat the oil and gently fry the paste, onion and garlic for 5 minutes.

2 Add the potatoes and butternut squash, and stir-fry for 2 minutes.

3 Add the rest of the ingredients, bring to the boil, cover, reduce the heat and simmer for 25 minutes.

4 With a sharp knife, check that the vegetables are tender. Serve.

Vegetarian Goulash (By-election Slops)

This is one of those classic student dishes that is trotted out time and time again, as it is easy to make and also cheap to serve to large numbers of people. The reason for the title is that I first experienced it when we were having a late-night meal while waiting for some important by-election results. Strangely, I don't remember anything about the by-election, just the meal. This goulash was followed by extremely, and I do mean extremely, runny brie!

SERVES 4–6 • PREP 20 min • COOKING 40 min

INGREDIENTS

1.25kg mixed vegetables,
  such as carrots, courgettes,
  potatoes, aubergines, mushrooms

3 tablespoons oil

2 onions, chopped

2 cloves garlic, crushed

400g can chopped tomatoes

1 red pepper, chopped

1 green pepper, chopped

4 tablespoons tomato purée

2 tablespoons paprika

salt and pepper

METHOD

1 Preheat the oven to 190°C/375°F/Gas 5.

2 Cut the vegetables into bite-sized pieces.

3 Heat the oil in a pan and fry the onions and garlic for
5 minutes.

4 Mix with the remaining ingredients and seasonings and
transfer to a casserole dish.

5 Bake in the preheated oven for 40 minutes or until all
the vegetables are cooked.

Vegetarian Cassoulet

SERVES 4 • PREP 15 min • COOKING 60 min

INGREDIENTS

3 tablespoons oil

2 onions, chopped

4 cloves garlic, crushed

2 x 400g cans cannellini beans, drained

2 tablespoons soft brown sugar

2 tablespoons wine vinegar

1 tablespoon treacle

1 tablespoon mustard

1 teaspoon chilli powder

250ml boiling water

FOR THE MEAN BUTTER

2 tablespoons butter, softened

2 tablespoons French mustard

2 tablespoons fresh parsley, chopped

2 cloves garlic, crushed

METHOD

1 Preheat the oven to 180°C/350°F/Gas 4.

2 Heat the oil in a pan and fry the onions and garlic for 10 minutes.

3 Add them, with the remaining ingredients (except for those for mean butter), to a casserole dish – do not cover with a lid.

4 Cook in the preheated oven for 1 hour.

5 Just before serving, mix the mean butter ingredients together and stir into the casserole.

Sue's Vegetarian Chilli

My memories of the origins of this dish are vague. I do know it had something to do with watching a horse race – the Grand National? – but all I really remember is we sat on the floor with a large saucepan in the middle, helping ourselves and smothering the chilli in sour cream and tortilla chips.

SERVES 5–6 • PREP 15 min • COOKING 30 min

INGREDIENTS

oil for frying
1 large onion, chopped
2 cloves garlic, crushed
1 aubergine, diced
1 green pepper, diced
2 carrots, sliced
150g mushrooms, sliced
2 x 400g cans tomatoes
2 x 400g cans beans in chilli sauce
3 tablespoons tomato purée
1–3 teaspoons chilli powder, to taste
salt and pepper

METHOD

1 Heat a little oil in a pan and fry the vegetables until soft.

2 Add the tomatoes, beans, tomato purée, and the chilli powder, season and simmer gently for 30 minutes.

3 Serve with rice or sour cream and tortilla chips.

Imam Bayildi (The Priest Fainted)

This is a dish that we discovered in Turkey and that I frequently make during the summer months. Serve with lots of crusty French bread to mop up the juices.

SERVES 4 • PREP 20 min • COOKING 45 min

INGREDIENTS

1 tablespoon olive oil, plus more
  for frying and drizzling
1 onion, chopped
2 cloves garlic, crushed
1 aubergine, cut into slices lengthways
400g can chopped tomatoes
2 tablespoons tomato purée
2 tablespoons fresh parsley, chopped

METHOD

1　Preheat the oven to 180°C/350°F/Gas 4.

2　Heat 1 tablespoon oil in a pan and fry the onion and garlic until soft.

3　Put them in a casserole dish.

4　Cover the bottom of the pan with oil and fry the aubergine slices, a few at a time, transferring them to the casserole dish as they brown. (You will need a lot of oil for this.)

5　Then add the remaining ingredients and bake in the preheated oven for 45 minutes.

6　Leave to cool.

7　Drizzle with more oil just before serving.

Winter Warmer

SERVES 4–6 • PREP 25 min • COOKING 40–50 min

INGREDIENTS

700g potatoes, thickly sliced
2 tablespoons oil
2 onions, peeled and cut into rings
1 tablespoon demerara sugar
1 teaspoon white wine vinegar
2 x 400g cans frankfurters, drained and sliced
400g can butter beans, drained
2 tablespoons wholegrain mustard
150ml crème fraîche

METHOD

1 Preheat the oven to 190°C/375°F/Gas 5.

2 Cook the potatoes in boiling water for just 5 minutes, then drain well.

3 Meanwhile, heat 1 tablespoon of oil and fry the onions for a few minutes until they are soft and starting to brown.

4 Add the sugar and vinegar and continue to cook until the onions are a deep brown colour. Mix together the onions, frankfurters, butter beans, mustard and crème fraîche and place in an ovenproof dish.

5 Gently mix the remaining oil with the potato slices and use those to cover the dish.

6 Bake in the preheated oven for 40–50 minutes until the top is golden brown.

PIZZA AND PASTA

Pizza Dough

ENOUGH TO MAKE 1 x 30cm PIZZA • PREP 10 mins + RISING TIME

INGREDIENTS

200g strong white bread flour
1 teaspoon salt
1 teaspoon sugar
1 teaspoon easy blend yeast
1 teaspoon oil
125ml hand-hot water

METHOD

1 Mix all the dry ingredients together with the oil, add the water, then knead for 5 minutes.

2 Leave the dough to rise in a covered bowl for 45 minutes.

3 Before using the dough, knead it once more until smooth.

Tomato Sauce (for Pizza and Pasta)

**MAKES ENOUGH TO COVER 1 x 30cm PIZZA •
PREP 5 min • COOKING 15–20 min**

INGREDIENTS

1 tablespoon oil
1 garlic clove, crushed
400g can chopped tomatoes
1 tablespoon tomato purée

METHOD

1 Heat the oil in a pan and gently fry the garlic for 1 minute.

2 Add the remaining ingredients, cover and simmer gently for 5 minutes to make a tomato sauce you can use in pasta dishes. Or simmer for 15–20 minutes for a thick sauce you can use for pizza.

Tip For pizza, the sauce should be thick enough so that, when a spoon is pushed through it, you can see the bottom of the pan and the sauce remains separated.

Pizza with Peppers and Mushrooms

SERVES 2–4 • PREP 15 min • COOKING 12–15 min

INGREDIENTS

Pizza Dough (page 243)
Tomato Sauce (page 244)
several thin slices green pepper
several thin slices red pepper
50g mushrooms, chopped
2 spring onions, sliced
50g mozzarella cheese, grated
salt and pepper
sprinkling of chilli flakes

METHOD

1 Preheat the oven to 230°C/450°F/Gas 8.

2 Roll out the dough into a 30cm circle.

3 Place on a large baking sheet and prick all over with a fork.

4 Spread with the tomato sauce.

5 Arrange the vegetables on top and sprinkle with the cheese.

6 Season to taste with salt, pepper and chilli flakes.

7 Bake in the preheated oven for 12–15 minutes.

Pizza Casa

This simple pizza is our favourite house pizza.

SERVES 2–4 • PREP 10 min • COOKING 12–15 min

INGREDIENTS

Pizza Dough (page 243)
Tomato Sauce (page 244)
several basil leaves, shredded
4 sun-dried tomatoes, sliced
75g mozzarella, sliced
salt and pepper

METHOD

1 Preheat the oven to 200°C/400°F/Gas 6.

2 Roll out the dough into a 30cm circle.

3 Place on a large baking sheet and prick all over with a fork.

4 Spread with the tomato sauce.

5 Arrange the basil leaves and sun-dried tomatoes on top and sprinkle with the cheese.

6 Season with salt and pepper.

7 Bake in the preheated oven for 12–15 minutes.

Tomato and Aubergine Sauce (for Pasta)

SERVES 4 • PREP 20 min • COOKING 30 min

INGREDIENTS

1 onion, chopped
2 cloves garlic, crushed
3 tablespoons oil
1 aubergine, diced
400g can chopped tomatoes
1 tablespoon tomato purée
sprinkling of oregano
salt and pepper

METHOD

1 Fry the onion and garlic in 1 tablespoon of the oil for 5 minutes, add the aubergine and the remaining oil and continue to cook until it is soft (5–10 minutes).

2 Add the rest of the ingredients and seasoning and simmer gently for 30 minutes.

3 Serve with pasta.

Pasta Primavera

SERVES 4 • PREP 40 min • COOKING 15 min

INGREDIENTS

300g broad beans, podded
200g fresh peas, podded
150g asparagus tips, each cut into 3 lengths
200g fine beans, each cut into 3 lengths
330g pasta
150ml double cream
salt and pepper
60g Parmesan cheese,
   freshly grated, and extra to serve

METHOD

1 Bring a saucepan full of water to the boil and then add the vegetables. As soon as the water returns to the boil, reduce the heat and time it for 4 minutes.

2 Drain the vegetables in a sieve and run cold water through it to stop them from cooking any further.

3 Put your pasta on to cook as directed on the packet.

4 Three minutes before it will be ready, put the cream in a large frying pan and let it simmer.

5 Place the vegetables in the cream. When the pasta is cooked, drain it well and mix it into the cream and vegetables.

6 Season well and stir in the Parmesan.

7 Serve immediately with extra Parmesan.

Roman Gnocchi (Semolina)

**SERVES 2 • PREP 20 min • COOKING 25–30 min +
STANDING TIME**

INGREDIENTS

275ml milk
salt and pepper
75g semolina
25g butter, softened
25g Parmesan cheese, grated
1 egg yolk, beaten
50g Cheddar cheese, grated

METHOD

1 In a medium saucepan, heat the milk to boiling point,
then add a good pinch of salt and pepper. When you can
see bubbles in the milk, start sprinkling in the semolina
and stir continuously with a wooden spoon. As it boils,
the semolina will thicken quickly; keep stirring
vigorously until it is so thick that the wooden spoon will
stay upright if left. (This takes about 2 minutes.)

2 Take the pan off the heat and beat in half of the butter
and the Parmesan cheese; next beat in the egg yolk.

3 Put some foil or greaseproof paper on a flat plate and
press the semolina down on to this to make a rough
square about 18 x 18cm. Put it in the fridge for an hour.

4 When you are ready to cook the semolina, heat the oven
to 200°C/400°F/Gas 6.

(continued over)

5 Butter a medium ovenproof dish, then spread the rest of the softened butter over the semolina mixture. Cut it into 8 triangles. Carefully transfer the triangles to the dish and cover with the Cheddar.

6 Bake for 25–30 minutes until it is golden brown and starting to crisp at the edges.

7 Let it stand for 5 minutes before serving.

CHICKEN DISHES

Chicken Enchiladas

SERVES 4 • PREP 20 min • COOKING 15 min

INGREDIENTS

FOR THE ENCHILADA SAUCE

500ml passata
1 teaspoon mild chilli powder
½ teaspoon cumin

FOR THE ENCHILADAS

2 tablespoons oil
2 large chicken breasts (approx 350–400g), boned and
  skinned and cut into large strips
1 onion, sliced
1 red pepper, deseeded and sliced
2 cloves garlic, crushed
1 red chilli, sliced (optional –
  only if you like it spicy)
8 small soft tortillas
150ml sour cream
150g Cheddar cheese, grated

(continued over)

METHOD

1 Preheat the oven to 180°C/350°F/Gas 4.

2 Put the sauce ingredients into a pan, cover and simmer together for about 10 minutes to make the sauce.

3 Heat the oil in a frying pan and stir-fry the chicken, onion, pepper, garlic and chilli (if using) for 5–8 minutes until the chicken is cooked and the vegetables have softened. Mix in 2 tablespoons of the enchilada sauce.

4 Lay out your tortillas and divide half of the enchilada sauce among them. Top with the chicken mixture.

5 Put some sour cream and a small sprinkling of cheese on the chicken and then roll the tortilla up tightly and place in an ovenproof dish (join side down). Do this with each tortilla.

6 Spoon the rest of the sauce over the tortillas and sprinkle with the remaining cheese.

7 Bake for 15 minutes until everything is warmed through and the cheese has melted.

Chicken Burritos

SERVES 4 • PREP 35 min • COOKING 30 min

INGREDIENTS

1 tablespoon oil
400g diced chicken
1 large onion, chopped
1 green pepper
2 large tomatoes, deseeded and flesh chopped
2 cloves garlic, crushed
100ml water
215g can spicy refried beans
4 large tortillas
guacamole to serve
sour cream to serve
salsa to serve

METHOD

1 Heat the oil in a saucepan with a tight-fitting lid. Add the chicken, onion, pepper, tomatoes and garlic. Quickly stir-fry for 2 minutes, then add the water and cover tightly.

2 Cook over a very low heat for 15 minutes. After 5 minutes, check nothing is sticking to the pan. Add a little more water if needed.

3 Warm up the beans and the tortillas as directed on the packet. (The tortillas can be done in the microwave, in a frying pan or wrapped in foil in the oven.)

(continued over)

4 Pick out the pieces of chicken and remove them to a plate. Using 2 forks, shred the chicken. Put it back in the pan and heat it through gently.

5 Spread out the tortillas and place some refried beans on each, then divide the chicken among them.

6 You can now add a little guacamole, sour cream and salsa to each.

7 Roll up each tortilla, tuck the sides in first and then fold it over to make the classic burrito shape. Serve with the rest of the guacamole, sour cream and salsa on the side.

Chicken Korma

SERVES 4 • PREP 20 min • COOKING 40 min

INGREDIENTS

2 tablespoons oil

4 chicken leg portions,
    each divided into a thigh
    and drumstick portion

1 large onion, chopped

2 teaspoons minced ginger

2 cloves garlic, crushed

1 tablespoon coriander

1 teaspoon turmeric

1 teaspoon garam masala

200ml coconut cream

200ml hot water

juice of ½ lemon

2 tablespoons toasted almonds
    (optional)

METHOD

1   Preheat the oven to 180°C/350°F/Gas 4.

2   Heat the oil in a large frying pan and gently brown the
    chicken portions.

3   Put them in a large casserole dish.

4   Now cook the onion, ginger, garlic and spices in the
    same pan for a few minutes until the onion starts to
    soften.

(continued over)

5 Keeping the heat low, add the coconut cream and stir it into the mixture with the hot water.

6 Squeeze the lemon over the chicken and then pour the sauce all over the chicken in the casserole dish.

7 Cover it tightly and cook in the preheated oven for 40 minutes or until the chicken is cooked through.

Tandoori Chicken

SERVES 4 • PREP 5 min • COOKING 35 min

INGREDIENTS

8 chicken drumsticks
8 chicken thighs
1 tablespoon tikka spice powder
2 cloves garlic, crushed
1 tablespoon tomato purée
1 tablespoon lemon juice
75ml sour cream
salt and pepper

METHOD

1 Preheat the oven to its highest temperature.

2 Make deep slashes all over the chicken pieces.

3 Mix together all the rest of the ingredients in a bowl, then add the chicken and cover with the mixture.

4 Transfer to an ovenproof dish and cook in the preheated oven for 35 minutes until the chicken is well cooked and blackening.

TIP If you have time, once the chicken has been prepared for cooking, cover it and leave it in the fridge for a while to marinate. The chicken is lovely served with lemon wedges, tomato and onion slices and a crisp green salad.

West Country Chicken

SERVES 2 • PREP 10 min • COOKING 45–50 min

INGREDIENTS

25g butter, softened

2 tablespoons wholegrain mustard

*1 teaspoon Worcestershire sauce
(optional)*

*2 medium chicken breasts,
boned and skinned*

1 apple, cored, peeled and sliced

¼ Savoy cabbage, sliced

250ml bottle dry cider

METHOD

1 Preheat the oven to 190°C/375°F/Gas 5.

2 Combine the butter, mustard and Worcestershire sauce
(if using) and use this to coat the chicken breasts.

3 Put the apple and cabbage in an ovenproof dish and
place the chicken breasts on top.

4 Pour over the cider, cover with a lid and cook in the
preheated oven for 45–50 minutes.

X-tra Nice Chicken

SERVES 6 • PREP 15 min • COOKING 35 min

INGREDIENTS

2 tablespoons oil

6 medium chicken breasts,
  boned and skinned

knob of butter

6 tomatoes, chopped

1 tablespoon wholegrain mustard

150ml white wine or chicken stock,
  made with ½ stock cube and
  boiling water

2 tablespoons fresh tarragon, chopped

salt and black pepper

100ml crème fraîche

METHOD

1 Preheat the oven to 180°C/350°F/Gas 4.

2 Heat the oil in a frying pan and fry the chicken until browned.

3 Place it in an ovenproof dish.

4 Add the butter to the pan and fry the tomatoes for 3 minutes.

5 Stir in the mustard and wine or stock, bring to the boil and then pour the sauce over the chicken.

(continued over)

6 Sprinkle with the tarragon, season, then cover with a lid and cook for 35 minutes.

7 Stir in the crème fraîche just before serving.

TIP You can use chopped tarragon in a cheese and herb omelette.

CHICKEN POT PIE

Buy a puff pastry rolled sheet. Put this filling in an ovenproof dish (34 x 21cm) and cover with the pastry, firm down at the edges and brush with beaten egg. Bake at 220°C/425°F/Gas 7 for 20–25 minutes until it has risen and turned golden.

Pot-roasted Chicken

SERVES 4–6 • PREP 15 min • COOKING 90 min

INGREDIENTS

½ Savoy cabbage, sliced
1 large leek, sliced
1.7–2kg free-range chicken
1 chicken stock cube
300ml boiling water
sprinkling of dried thyme
25g butter

METHOD

1 Preheat the oven to 200°C/400°F/Gas 6.

2 Put the cabbage and leek in a large casserole dish and place the chicken on top.

3 Make up the chicken stock with the cube and boiling water, then add the thyme.

4 Pour the stock over the chicken and dot it with pieces of butter.

5 Cover and cook in the preheated oven for 1 hour.

6 Remove the cover and cook for another 30 minutes.

7 Divide the chicken and vegetables among the plates, spoon over the cooking liquid and serve.

(continued over)

TIP This is best served with baked potatoes, which have the bonus of being cooked alongside the chicken.

If you don't have a casserole dish with a lid, use a roasting tin and cover it with roasting foil.

Italian Garlic Chicken Casserole

SERVES 6 • PREP 15 min • COOKING 45–50 min

INGREDIENTS

6 chicken leg portions, divided into
  thighs and drumsticks
500g new potatoes, halved if large
1 onion, thickly sliced
2 carrots, roughly chopped
1 bulb of garlic, unpeeled
100ml olive oil
sprigs of fresh thyme
salt and black pepper
100ml crème fraîche (optional)

METHOD

1 Preheat the oven to 220°C/425°F/Gas 7.

2 Put all the ingredients (except the crème fraîche, if
  using) in a large roasting tin.

3 Mix well so that everything has a coating of oil.

4 Season, and cook in the preheated oven for 20 minutes.

5 Stir all the ingredients. Turn the heat down to
  180°C/350°F/Gas 4. Continue to cook for a further 20–30
  minutes until the chicken is cooked and the potatoes
  have browned.

6 If using the crème fraîche, stir it in just before serving.

Chicken and Chick Pea Stew

SERVES 4–6 • PREP 15 min • COOKING 60 min

INGREDIENTS

2 tablespoons oil

12 pieces mixed chicken
  thighs and drumsticks

2 large onions, chopped

4 cloves garlic, crushed

500g jar passata

4 teaspoons dried thyme

400g can chick peas, drained

salt and black pepper

METHOD

1 Preheat the oven to 190°C/375°F/Gas 5.

2 Heat half the oil in a pan and quickly fry the chicken
  pieces 6–8 at a time.

3 As each batch is browned, place it in an ovenproof dish.

4 Fry the onions in the rest of the oil until they start to
  brown, then add them to the dish.

5 Add the rest of the ingredients and season.

6 Cover and cook in the preheated oven for 1 hour.

TIP Don't crowd the chicken pieces when frying them – you want to
get them nice and golden.

Jambalaya

SERVES 6 • PREP 25 min • COOKING 15 min

INGREDIENTS

2 tablespoons oil

2 medium chicken breasts,
  boned and skinned, cut into cubes

150g chorizo sausage, salami type,
  skinned and sliced

½ tablespoon paprika

1 large onion, chopped

2 celery sticks, sliced

3 peppers of mixed colours,
  deseeded and cubed

4 cloves garlic, crushed

2 teaspoons minced chilli

350g long-grain rice

4 tomatoes, cut into wedges

1 litre chicken stock, made with
  1 stock cube and boiling water

METHOD

1 Heat the oil in a frying pan and fry the chicken, chorizo
   and paprika for a few minutes until the chicken starts
   to brown.

2 Remove the meat to a large saucepan.

3 Fry the onion, celery, peppers, garlic and chilli until soft
   and starting to brown.

(continued over)

4 Add this to the saucepan and start to heat through.

5 When hot, add the rice and stir it through.

6 Add the tomatoes and stock.

7 Bring to the boil, then simmer for 15 minutes until the stock is absorbed.

Moroccan Lemon Chicken with Olives

SERVES 6 • PREP 20 min + MARINATING TIME • COOKING 65 min

INGREDIENTS

MARINADE

2 tablespoons oil

6 chicken legs, divided into thighs
   and drumsticks

1 teaspoon cinnamon

2 teaspoons minced ginger

1 tablespoon runny honey

juice of 1 lemon

TO COOK

100ml wine

200ml chicken stock, made with
   1 stock cube and 200ml boiling water

1 lemon, cut into 8 wedges

100g mixed olives, stoned

black pepper

METHOD

1 The day before, put all the marinade ingredients in a covered bowl or a large bag and refrigerate.

2 When you are ready to cook, preheat the oven to 190°C/375°F/Gas 5.

(continued over)

3 Put the marinated mixture into a hobproof and ovenproof dish. Add the wine and stock and bring to the boil. Add the lemon, then cover and bake in the preheated oven for 30 minutes.

4 Use the stock to baste the chicken and return the dish to the oven uncovered for 20 minutes. Baste again and cook for a further 10 minutes.

5 Remove the chicken to a serving platter. Put the pan on the hob and bring the sauce up to a boil. Boil for a minute or two to thicken the sauce slightly.

6 Stir through the olives and season with black pepper before pouring the sauce over the chicken.

BEEF DISHES

Mince Bake with Cheesy Pasta Topping

SERVES 4 • PREP 25 min • COOKING 20 min

INGREDIENTS

1 tablespoon oil

1 large onion, chopped

2 cloves garlic, crushed

500g beef mince

330g dischi volanti pasta or
  other small pasta, such as
  macaroni or penne rigate

350–500ml tomato sauce for pasta (page 244)

350g cheese sauce, home made
  or bought

2 tablespoons Parmesan cheese,
  freshly grated

METHOD

1 Preheat the oven to 200°C/400°F/Gas 6.

2 Put the water on to boil for the pasta.

(continued over)

3 Heat the oil in a pan and cook the onion and garlic gently for 5 minutes.

4 Push the onion to the side of the pan, add the beef mince and fry until no signs of pink remain.

5 Put the pasta on to cook. Cook as directed on the packet.

6 Pour the tomato sauce into the mince and stir well. Simmer gently until the pasta is cooked.

7 When the pasta is cooked, drain it and mix it with the cheese sauce.

8 Put the meat sauce into an ovenproof dish and cover with the cheesy pasta.

9 Sprinkle with Parmesan and bake in the preheated oven for 20 minutes, until the cheese topping is browning.

TIP I buy dischi volanti pasta in Tesco but it can easily be substituted with many other types of pasta. This is one of those dishes that you can cook in many different ways: you can substitute lamb mince for the mince here, you can add other vegetables to make it go further – carrots, leeks, mushrooms, peas – or that old favourite, baked beans. I have even made it with canned beef and lamb mince. The varieties are endless, so make up your own.

Lasagne

SERVES 4 • PREP 30 min • COOKING 35–40 min

INGREDIENTS

1 tablespoon olive oil
1 large onion, chopped
2 cloves garlic, crushed
500g beef mince
2 tablespoons tomato purée
1 teaspoon dried oregano
400g can tomatoes
1 beef stock cube
150ml red wine or water
salt and pepper
12 lasagne sheets (not pre-cooked type)
350ml tub fresh cheese sauce
2 heaped tablespoons grated
  Parmesan cheese

METHOD

1 In a large frying pan, heat the oil and gently cook the onion and garlic for 5 minutes. Push the onion to the side of the pan and quickly cook the beef until no signs of pink remain.

2 Add the tomato purée and oregano and stir through. Add the tomatoes, sprinkle in the beef cube and add the red wine or water. Season.

(continued over)

3 Simmer gently for 15 minutes.

4 Meanwhile, preheat the oven to 190°C/375°F/Gas 5.

5 Put some boiling water into a shallow dish and place the lasagne sheets in the water, leaving them for a few minutes to soften slightly. Remove and pat dry.

6 When the meat sauce is ready, put ⅓ into the bottom of an ovenproof dish. Cover with a layer of four of the lasagne sheets.

7 Spoon over ⅓ of the cheese sauce.

8 Carry on alternating the layers, finishing with a layer of cheese sauce.

9 Sprinkle with the Parmesan and bake for 35–40 minutes until well browned on top.

VEGETARIAN LASAGNE

Use 350ml cheese sauce. Put a little of the Ratatouille from page 224 in the bottom of your lasagne dish, cover with a layer of the lasagne sheets, then some cheese sauce. Carry on layering your dish, finishing with a layer of cheese sauce. Sprinkle the cheese on top and then bake as above.

Mince, Baked Bean and Potato Pie

SERVES 4 • PREP 20 min • COOKING 60 min

INGREDIENTS

2 tablespoons oil
1 large onion, chopped
2 large carrots, roughly chopped
500g beef mince
100g frozen peas
300ml beef gravy, made with
   6 heaped teaspoons gravy granules
1 teaspoon dried mixed herbs
   or fresh thyme
400g baked beans
dash of Worcestershire sauce
2 baking potatoes, unpeeled
   and thickly sliced
salt and pepper

METHOD

1 Preheat the oven to 200°C/400°F/Gas 6.

2 In a large frying pan, heat 1 tablespoon of the oil and gently fry the onion and carrots for 5 minutes.

3 Transfer them to a large casserole dish.

4 Now, on a high heat, fry the beef mince so that you get lots of brown bits.

(continued over)

5 Add the peas, beef gravy and herbs. Mix them into the meat, then add the beans and Worcestershire sauce and stir through thoroughly.

6 Add this to the casserole dish and stir.

7 In a bowl, mix the sliced potato with the other tablespoon of oil and season.

8 Cover the top of the casserole with the potato and cook in the preheated oven for 1 hour or until the potato is crispy on top.

Bobotie

SERVES 4 • PREP 20 min • COOKING 30 min

INGREDIENTS

1 tablespoon oil

1 onion, chopped

2 cloves garlic, crushed

2 heaped tablespoons mild
  curry paste

500g beef mince

2 tablespoons tomato purée

1 tablespoon white wine vinegar
  or lemon juice

2 heaped tablespoons sultanas

1 slice bread, crusts removed
  and soaked in 3 tablespoons milk,
  mashed

1 banana, mashed

salt and pepper

2 eggs, beaten

200ml milk

METHOD

1 Preheat the oven to 180°C/350°F/Gas 4.

2 Heat the oil and fry the onion and garlic until they start
   to brown.

3 Add the curry paste and beef and stir-fry until the
   mince has browned.

(continued over)

4 Add the tomato purée, vinegar or lemon juice, sultanas, mashed bread and banana.

5 Season and transfer to an ovenproof dish.

6 Mix together the eggs and milk, season and pour over the meat mixture.

7 Bake in the preheated oven for 30 minutes or until the egg mixture has set.

Beef Stew

SERVES 8 • PREP 45 min • COOKING 180 min

INGREDIENTS

4 onions, finely sliced

4 cloves garlic, crushed

4 tablespoons oil

1.5kg lean stewing beef, cubed

4 tablespoons flour

4 carrots, halved and sliced thickly

200g butternut squash (1 squash),
  flesh diced

1 tablespoon tomato purée

1 tablespoon soft brown sugar

2 tablespoons wholegrain mustard

1 litre brown ale

1 beef stock cube, crumbled

1 teaspoon mixed herbs or
  a few sprigs of fresh thyme

METHOD

1 Preheat the oven to 170°C/325°F/Gas 3.

2 Fry the onion and garlic in 2 tablespoons of oil until
   brown, then remove them to a large casserole dish that
   can also be used on the hob.

3 Put the meat and the flour in a large bowl and mix well.
   Fry in 3 batches until brown, then place in the casserole
   dish.

(continued over)

4 Add the carrots and butternut squash. Mix the rest of the ingredients together and pour them over the meat.

5 Put the casserole dish on the hob and bring it up to a gentle simmer – don't boil as it toughens the meat. Cover and cook in the preheated oven for 2 hours, give it a good stir and put it back in for another 30–60 minutes, until the meat is lovely and tender.

TIP   This recipe makes 8 servings. I suggest that you use half as a beef stew and serve it with jacket potatoes or mash.

STEAK PIE

Buy some puff pastry, put the beef stew in an ovenproof dish and top with the pastry, brush with beaten egg and cook in a preheated oven (220°C/425°F/Gas 7) until the pastry is well risen and brown.

BEEF CARBONNADE

Again, put the beef stew in an ovenproof dish, heat through in a hot oven and then take slices of French bread, dip them in the meat juices, turn them over and lay them on the top of the dish. Bake uncovered for 15 minutes until the bread topping is crisp.

ROASTS

Stuffed Nut Roast

SERVES 6 • PREP 30 min • COOKING 70 min + COOLING TIME

INGREDIENTS

FOR THE NUTMEAT

100g pine nuts
50g cashews
1 onion, chopped
25g butter
50g ground almonds
60ml milk
2 eggs, beaten
100g wholemeal breadcrumbs
salt and pepper

FOR THE STUFFING

113g sachet stuffing mix
100g mushrooms, chopped
25g butter
1 clove garlic, crushed
dash of soy sauce
pinch of mixed herbs

(continued over)

METHOD

1 Preheat the oven to 190°C/375°F/Gas 5.

2 Grease an 800g loaf tin very well.

3 Put the pine nuts and cashews in a bag and bash them with a heavy object (e.g. a can of soup) until the nuts have broken into very small pieces.

4 Fry the onion for 5 minutes in the butter, then mix in all the nutmeat ingredients together.

5 Put half of the mixture into the tin and press down.

6 Make up the stuffing as directed on the packet.

7 Cook the mushrooms in the butter for a few minutes until soft.

8 Mix all the stuffing ingredients together and layer it over the nutmeat.

9 Level and then cover with the remaining nutmeat, level and cover with foil.

10 Cook for 1 hour, then remove the foil and cook for a further 10 minutes to brown.

11 Cool in the tin for 10–15 minutes before turning it out.

Roast Chicken

**SERVES 4–6 • PREP 5 min • COOKING 60–90 min +
RESTING TIME**

INGREDIENTS

1.5–2kg roasting chicken
lemon, halved
oil for basting
salt and pepper

METHOD

1 Preheat the oven to 190°C/375°F/Gas 5.

2 Remove any giblets from the chicken.

3 Rinse the bird and pat it dry.

4 Place the halved lemon inside the chicken.

5 Brush it with oil and season.

6 Place the chicken in a roasting tin and cook for
   1–1½ hours.

7 To check whether it's ready, prick the flesh in a few
   places so that the juices run out. If there are any signs
   of pink, cook it for longer.

8 Let it rest for 10 minutes before carving.

Roast Pork

SERVES 6 • PREP 5 min • COOKING 105 min + RESTING TIME

INGREDIENTS

1.25kg roasting joint of pork
  (loin, leg or shoulder), pre-scored
oil for basting
salt and pepper

METHOD

1 Preheat the oven to 190°C/375°F/Gas 5.

2 Rinse the joint and pat it dry.

3 Brush it with oil and season.

4 Place the joint in a roasting tin and cook for 30 minutes.

5 Continue to cook for 30 minutes per 500g. So, for a 1.25kg joint, cook for a total time of 1 hour and 45 minutes.

6 If very crisp crackling is required, turn up the heat as much as possible for the last 15 minutes of the cooking time.

7 Leave the meat to rest for 10 minutes.

8 Remove the crackling before carving.

9 Serve crackling on the side.

Roast Lamb

SERVES 6 • PREP 5 min • COOKING 70 min + RESTING TIME

INGREDIENTS

1.25kg joint of lamb (leg or shoulder)
oil for basting
salt and pepper
rosemary, chopped (optional)

METHOD

1 Preheat the oven to 190°C/375°F/Gas 5.

2 Rinse the joint and pat it dry.

3 Brush it with oil and season. Sprinkle with chopped rosemary (if using).

4 Put the joint in a roasting tin and cook for 25 minutes.

5 Continue to cook for 20 minutes per 500g. So, for a 1.25kg joint, cook for a total time of 1 hour and 10 minutes. (Cook for 10–15 minutes longer if you like your meat well done.)

7 Leave the meat to rest for 10 minutes before carving.

Roast Beef

SERVES 6 • PREP 5 min • COOKING 50–70 min + RESTING TIME

INGREDIENTS

1kg beef roasting joint
oil for basting
salt and pepper
mustard powder and flour
    (optional)

METHOD

1 Preheat the oven to 220°C/425°F/Gas 7.

2 Rinse the joint and pat it dry.

3 Brush it with oil and season.

4 Sprinkle with a little mustard powder and flour
   (if using).

5 Place the joint in a roasting pan and cook for
   20 minutes.

6 Turn the heat down to 190°C/375°F/Gas 5 and roast for
   another 30 minutes for rare, 40 minutes for medium
   rare or 50 minutes for well-done meat.

7 Leave the meat to rest for 10 minutes before carving.

5 Serve with . . .

In everyday student cooking, it is unusual to have a main meal accompanied by vegetables. It is much more common to include vegetables in the dish being cooked. However, there will always be times when you do want to cook some vegetables separately – if you are getting together with some friends to produce a Sunday lunch, for instance.

Here is a little information on how to cook some of those staples, such as vegetables, rice, couscous and potatoes. If you buy pre-packed vegetables in a supermarket, these often include instructions on how to cook them. It is, of course, usually much cheaper to buy vegetables loose, so here is how to cook the most popular ones. I've also included some tasty salads and dressings.

It is also useful to know how to jazz up a simple meal just by serving a special rice or potato dish. And although you can buy some very good fresh cheese sauces now, it is still usually cheaper to make your own.

THE CHOICES:

Broad Beans

Broccoli

Brussels Sprouts

Roasted Butternut Squash

Cabbage

Carrots

Cauliflower

Stir-fried Celery and Walnuts

Stir-fried Courgettes

Couscous

Couscous with Fruit and Nuts

French Beans

Garlic Bread

Stir-fried Greens

Creamed Leeks

Onion Gravy

Butter-fried Parsnip

Roasted Honey-glazed Parsnips

Pasta

Fresh Peas

Baby Potatoes and Peas

Baked Potatoes

Mashed Potato

Oven Chips

Patatas Bravas

Potato Skins

Potatoes in Red Pesto

Roast Potatoes

Roasted New Potatoes

Wedgy Potatoes

Basmati Rice

Runner Beans

Sweet Potato Baked in Foil

Egg-fried Rice

Chinese Egg-fried Rice

Pilau Rice

Salad Dressing

French Dressing

Carrot Salad

Pan-fried Tomato and Pepper
Salad

Garlic Mushroom Salad

Mustard-dressed Mixed Salad

Side Salad

Salad with Banana Dressing

Tabbouleh

Apple Sauce

Cheese Sauce

Cranberry Sauce with Lime
and Ginger

Fruity Curry Sauce

Quick Creamy Curry Sauce

Quick Chilli 'n' Tomato Sauce

Salsa

Yorkshire Puddings

Broad Beans

SERVES 1 • PREP 15 min

INGREDIENTS

150–200g broad beans

METHOD

1 Split each pod and remove the beans. Discard the pods.

2 In a medium saucepan, bring some water to the boil.

3 Add the beans to the water and when the water has reached boiling point, cook for 4 minutes.

4 Drain and run the beans under cold water to stop them cooking.

5 It will now be easy to remove the grey outer shell, leaving a lovely bright green bean. These are lovely in salads or serve them as a vegetable accompaniment to your main meal.

Broccoli

SERVES 1 • PREP 10 min

INGREDIENTS

80–100g broccoli

METHOD

1 Cut off the florets and divide them into bite-sized pieces.

2 Broccoli can be boiled but is best steamed. Bring a pan of water to the boil, then put your broccoli florets in a steamer and place it over the boiling water.

3 Cook for 7–8 minutes or until a knife tip easily pierces the stem.

4 Serve as a vegetable accompaniment.

TIP Broccoli also makes a great salad served with a little sesame oil drizzled over it and some chopped red chilli sprinkled on top.

Brussels Sprouts

SERVES 1 • PREP 10 min

INGREDIENTS

80g Brussels sprouts

METHOD

1 Remove any discoloured outer leaves and cut off the very bottom of the stem.

2 Sprouts can be boiled or steamed. Bring a pan of water to the boil and either place the sprouts in the boiling water or add them to a steamer and place that over the boiling water.

3 Cook for about 8 minutes or until a knife tip easily pierces the stem.

4 Drain and serve as an accompaniment to your main meal.

TIP For a special occasion cook some cubed bacon or pancetta and stir with butter into the sprouts.

Roasted Butternut Squash

SERVES 4 • PREP 5 min • COOKING 35 min

INGREDIENTS

1 *butternut squash*
4 *tablespoons soft brown sugar*
4 *tablespoons oil*
salt and pepper

METHOD

1 Preheat the oven to 180°C/350°F/Gas 4.

2 Peel the butternut squash with a potato peeler.

3 Remove the seeds and roughly chop the flesh into chunks about 3cm long.

4 Put the chunks into a bowl with the sugar and oil and season.

5 With your hands, rub the sugar and seasoned oil into the flesh.

6 Put some foil on a baking tray and then tumble the squash on to this and spread it out.

7 Roast in the preheated oven for about 35 minutes until the squash is cooked through.

TIP   I sometimes vary this by adding a little curry powder with the seasoned oil; at other times, I use a little chopped sage.

Cabbage

SERVES 4 • PREP 10 min

INGREDIENTS

1 cabbage
large knob of butter
salt and pepper

METHOD

1 Remove any large outer leaves and discard.

2 Cut in quarters lengthways.

3 Cut away any large stalks.

4 Now gather the leaves together and cut them into thin shreds.

5 Wash thoroughly and place the cabbage, without draining it, in a large pan.

6 Cover and cook over a high heat for 3–4 minutes. (Be careful that the pan does not run dry – add a little more boiling water if necessary.)

7 Drain and then return the cabbage to the pan and add the butter and seasoning. Continue to heat until the butter melts.

Carrots

SERVES 2 • PREP 15 min

INGREDIENTS

160–200g carrots
  (about 3 carrots, depending on size)

METHOD

1. Peel the carrots as thinly as possible (this is so much easier with a potato peeler and they are really cheap to buy).

2. Cut off the top of each carrot, and the bottom if it looks ropy.

3. Slice each carrot into rounds or cut it in half lengthways and slice into matchsticks.

4. Now boil or steam the carrots for about 12 minutes or until the point of a knife goes into the carrot easily.

TIP Whole baby carrots are usually not peeled. If bought with the green fronds still on, cut the greenery off very near to the top of the carrot, but leave a little of the stalk, which can be eaten. They will take 12–15 minutes to cook through – test with a knife tip to check whether they are ready to serve.

Cauliflower

SERVES 4 • PREP 10–15 min

INGREDIENTS

1 cauliflower

METHOD

1 Cut off the tough stem and divide the florets into bite-sized pieces.

2 Cauliflower can be boiled or steamed, so boil some water and then either put the florets in a steamer and place it over the boiling water or add the cauliflower directly to the pan.

3 Cook for 6–8 minutes (or for about 10–12 minutes if you like your cauliflower softer).

4 Check with a knife tip before serving.

TIP Cauliflower is often served with a cheese sauce that can be made (see page 337) or bought.

CAULIFLOWER CHEESE

Mix the cooked cauliflower with cheese sauce, put it in a heatproof dish and scatter grated cheese over the top. Cook in a hot oven or under a grill until the cheese is bubbling and brown.

Stir-fried Celery and Walnuts

SERVES 6 • PREP 5 min

INGREDIENTS

knob of butter

*1 bunch of celery, trimmed
and chopped diagonally*

75g walnut pieces

2 tablespoons demerara sugar

METHOD

1 Melt the butter and stir-fry the celery for 2 minutes.

2 Add the walnuts and sugar and stir until the sugar caramelises.

TIP This is excellent as an accompaniment to any roasted or grilled meats or poultry.

Stir-fried Courgettes

SERVES 6 • PREP 10 min

INGREDIENTS

3 tablespoons oil

2 large or 4 medium courgettes, sliced

3 garlic cloves, crushed

1 bunch of spring onions, sliced

salt and black pepper

METHOD

1   Heat the oil in a frying pan and fry the courgettes and garlic for 5 minutes until they start to brown.

2   Add the spring onions and stir-fry for another 2 minutes.

3   Season and serve.

Couscous

SERVES 4 • PREP 15 min

INGREDIENTS

200ml vegetable stock, made
  with ½ stock cube and
  boiling water
150g couscous
knob of butter
1 tablespoon raisins
1 tablespoon toasted
  flaked almonds

METHOD

1 Place the stock in a saucepan and bring it to the boil.
   Add the couscous and stir.

2 Remove the pan from the heat, cover and allow it to
   stand for 5 minutes until the stock is absorbed. Add the
   butter, fork it through, re-cover the pan and let it stand
   for another 5 minutes.

3 Fork through the couscous to separate the grains. Add
   the raisins and almonds before serving.

Couscous with Fruit and Nuts

SERVES 6 • PREP 20 min

INGREDIENTS

240ml vegetable stock,
  made with 1 stock cube and
  boiling water
2 tablespoons olive oil
200g couscous
salt
100g sultanas
100g semi-dried, ready-to-eat apricots,
  chopped
50g toasted flaked almonds
black pepper

METHOD

1 Put the hot stock and oil in a medium saucepan. Bring to the boil and add the couscous and a pinch of salt. Stir, cover and turn the heat off.

2 Leave the couscous to stand for 10 minutes, then stir, re-cover the pan and leave it for another 5 minutes to finish cooking.

3 Mix in the rest of the ingredients, season (only add more salt if needed) and serve.

French Beans

SERVES 1 • PREP 10 min

INGREDIENTS

80–100g French beans

METHOD

1 These can be bought trimmed and ready for cooking, but if you are buying them loose all you need to do is to cut off both ends (this is called 'topping and tailing' them).

2 Then either boil or steam the beans for 5–8 minutes depending on how thick they are and how you prefer them cooked.

3 Check with a knife tip before serving.

CHINESE SESAME BEANS

Serve the cooked beans with some toasted sesame seeds and a drizzle of sesame oil and soy sauce. This makes a lovely accompaniment to Chinese dishes.

Garlic Bread

SERVES 4–6 • PREP 5 min • COOKING 20–30 min

INGREDIENTS

1 French loaf
100g butter, softened
mixed herbs
2 cloves garlic, crushed
poppy seeds (optional)

METHOD

1 Preheat the oven to 200°C/400°F/Gas 6.

2 Slice the loaf at about 2.5cm intervals to within 1cm of the base.

3 Mix together the butter, herbs and garlic and spread the mixture into the cuts.

4 Smear a little butter over the top of the loaf and sprinkle with poppy seeds (if using).

5 Wrap the bread in foil and cook in the preheated oven for 20–30 minutes. Serve hot.

Stir-fried Greens

SERVES 4 • PREP 10 min

INGREDIENTS

2 tablespoons oil
½ Savoy cabbage, shredded
250g spinach, shredded
  if large-leaved
2 cloves garlic, crushed
2 teaspoons minced ginger
2 tablespoons soy sauce

METHOD

1 Heat the oil in a frying pan and stir-fry the cabbage, spinach and garlic until the spinach is just starting to wilt.

2 Add the ginger and soy sauce, stir through and serve.

Creamed Leeks

SERVES 4 • PREP 15 min

INGREDIENTS

4 leeks
1 onion
several sprigs of thyme or
  a few leaves of sage (optional)
40g butter
150ml double cream
salt and pepper

METHOD

1 First prepare the leeks and onion.

2 Cut the top and roots off the leeks and onion.

3 Remove any coarse leaves from the leek and peel off the onion skin.

4 Wash the leek thoroughly, as grit can hide within the leaves.

5 Slice the leek thinly and cut the onion in half and then slice it thinly.

6 If using the fresh herbs, strip the thyme leaves from the stems or finely slice the sage leaves.

7 Now melt the butter in a large frying pan and add the vegetables and herbs (if using).

8 Fry gently for 5 minutes and then add the cream and cook for a few more minutes until the sauce has reduced. Season to taste.

TIP For a 'slimmer' version of this dish, you can use chicken or vegetable stock instead of cream.

CHEESY CREAMED LEEKS

Transfer the vegetables to a heatproof dish, scatter grated cheese on top and then cook in a hot oven or under a grill until the cheese is bubbling and brown.

Onion Gravy

SERVES 4–6 • PREP 15 min

INGREDIENTS

large knob of butter
2 onions, finely chopped
½ teaspoon caster sugar
1 tablespoon cornflour
½ teaspoon Marmite
pepper

METHOD

1 Melt the butter in a frying pan and gently fry the onions for about 5 minutes until they soften and start to brown.

2 Add the sugar and stir through – this will help to caramelise the onions.

3 Mix the cornflour with a little water to make a paste, then make up to 500ml with boiling water.

4 Mix in the Marmite.

5 Pour the liquid into the onions and bring it to the boil.

6 Season with pepper and simmer for 5–10 minutes until the gravy is to your taste.

TIP This makes about 300ml when I make it, but the amount will depend on how long you cook it for and how fast. If you like your gravy a little darker, you can add a drop or two of gravy browning.

Butter-fried Parsnip

SERVES 1 • PREP 20 min

INGREDIENTS

1 large parsnip
several sprigs of thyme or
  a few leaves of sage (optional)
large knob of butter
1 teaspoon oil
salt and pepper

METHOD

1　Peel the parsnip thinly. A potato peeler is useful here.

2　Top and tail, then cut into 6 pieces of equal thickness.

3　If you are using the fresh herbs, strip the thyme leaves from the stalks or finely slice the sage leaves.

4　Heat the butter and oil in a large frying pan until the butter melts.

5　Add the parsnip and herbs (if using), turn up the heat a little and cook for about 10–15 minutes until the parsnip is tender, turns golden and starts to crisp.

Roasted Honey-glazed Parsnips

SERVES 4–6 • PREP 10 min • COOKING 30–35 min

INGREDIENTS

3 large parsnips or 500g
  packet of parsnips
large knob of butter
salt and pepper
1½ tablespoons runny honey

METHOD

1 Preheat the oven to 190°C/375°F/Gas 5.

2 Cut each parsnip into four pieces. If the parsnips are very large and the core looks woody (has little holes), cut out the core.

3 Cut each quarter into 2 or 3 equal-sized pieces. In a frying pan or hobproof and ovenproof dish, melt the butter. Gently toss the parsnips in the butter to coat. Cook for 5 minutes. Season and transfer to the oven for 20 minutes.

4 Drizzle with the honey and turn so that it coats the parsnips.

5 Cook for 5–10 minutes until the parsnips are golden brown.

Pasta

SERVES 1 • PREP 15 min

INGREDIENTS

100g pasta
knob of butter or margarine
salt and black pepper

METHOD

1 Cook the pasta as directed on the packet (generally for 9–12 minutes), drain and mix in the butter or margarine.

2 Season well.

TIP When serving pasta as a side dish, tagliatelle is a good choice, but it is really up to you. If you are just cooking up some pasta to keep you going, any grated cheese makes a nice addition.

Fresh Peas

SERVES 1 • PREP 10 min

INGREDIENTS

200g fresh peas, bought weight

METHOD

1 Split each pod open over a basin.

2 Run your nail down the pod, shelling the peas into the basin.

3 Cook in boiling water for 10 minutes.

4 Try one and see if it is cooked to your liking; cook for longer if you wish.

TIP   Mint goes well with peas so sprinkle some over if you want.

Baby Potatoes and Peas

SERVES 2 • PREP 25 min

INGREDIENTS

250g baby new potatoes
80g sugarsnap peas
80g frozen peas
small knob of butter
salt and pepper

METHOD

1 Bring a saucepan of water to the boil and add the potatoes. Cook for about 15–20 minutes until they are really tender.

2 In a separate pan, boil some more water and add the sugarsnap peas and the frozen peas. Cook for 4 minutes.

3 When all the vegetables are cooked, drain them well and mix them together, adding just a little butter and seasoning. Serve.

Baked Potatoes

SERVES 1 • PREP 5 min • COOKING 60–90 min

INGREDIENTS

1 large potato, cleaned
knob of butter or margarine
salt and pepper

METHOD

1 Preheat the oven to 220°C/425°F/Gas 7.

2 Prick the potato all over with a fork.

3 Bake in the preheated oven for 1–1½ hours, depending on size.

4 Cut the potato in half and fork in the butter or margarine.

5 Season well. (Extra cash could buy cheese or baked beans to add as a filling.)

CHEESE AND MARMITE JACKETS

When the potato is cooked, scoop out the flesh, mix with butter or margarine, 1 teaspoon Marmite and 25g grated cheese. Preheat the grill. Put the skins on an ovenproof tray, fill with the potato mixture and grill until brown.

Mashed Potato

SERVES 4 • PREP 30 min

INGREDIENTS

800g potatoes, peeled and
  cut into chunks
50g butter
50ml milk
salt and black pepper

METHOD

1 Cook the potatoes in boiling water until tender (about 20 minutes), then drain well.

2 Mash with a potato masher or fork.

3 Gradually add the other ingredients and work them in.

4 Season and serve.

MASHED POTATO WITH GARLIC AND OLIVE OIL

Replace the butter and milk with 100ml olive oil and add 2 cloves of crushed garlic.

COLCANNON

Prepare and cook a small cabbage and then mix it into the mash just before serving. Chopped spring onions can also be added.

Oven Chips

SERVES 4 • PREP 10 min • COOKING 30–35 min

INGREDIENTS

4 x 250g potatoes, skins removed
2 tablespoons oil
salt

METHOD

1 Preheat the oven to 220°C/425°F/Gas 7.

2 Cut the potatoes into slices and then cut the slices into strips.

3 Put the potatoes into a saucepan with cold water and bring to the boil.

4 Cook for 3 minutes, then plunge the potatoes into cold water.

5 Drain and pat dry.

6 Mix with the oil and season with salt.

7 Place on a baking tray and cook in the preheated oven for 10 minutes.

8 Then turn the heat down to 180°C/350°F/Gas 4 and bake for a further 20–25 minutes until the chips have browned.

Patatas Bravas

If there is one dish that I absolutely could not live without, this is it. I like potato dishes and this one has a heavenly sauce. We are very keen tapas fans, although it's got to be said that there are some pretty ropy imitations of tapas bars around. There are also some real gems. Our favourite was in Brighton, Casa Don Carlos (run by Carlos, of course). His *patatas bravas* were great, as was everything on the menu. This is my version.

SERVES 2 • PREP 30 min

INGREDIENTS

300g new potatoes, unpeeled
oil for shallow frying

FOR THE SAUCE
2 tablespoons olive oil
1 tablespoon tomato purée
2 teaspoons wine vinegar
1 teaspoon paprika
1 tablespoon single cream (optional)
salt and pepper

METHOD

1 Boil the potatoes for 10–15 minutes until they are just tender but not soft.

2 Drain and cool, cut into halves or quarters depending on size.

(continued over)

3 Heat the oil and fry the potatoes until brown.

4 Mix the sauce ingredients together, season and pour the sauce over the potatoes. Serve.

Potato Skins

SERVES 4 • PREP 5 min • COOKING 20 min

INGREDIENTS

4 x 250g potatoes
2 tablespoons oil
2 tablespoons soy sauce
pinch of chilli powder

METHOD

1 Preheat the oven to 220°C/425°F/Gas 7.

2 Cut the skins from the potatoes thickly (the flesh can be used for oven chips or mash).

3 Mix the skins with the other ingredients.

4 Put the skins on a baking tray and cook in the preheated oven for about 20 minutes until they are crisp and brown.

5 Serve with a dip (sour cream is especially nice).

Potatoes in Red Pesto

SERVES 4 • PREP 20 min

INGREDIENTS

500g baby new potatoes,
  cooked and cooled
½ x 170g jar or
  carton fresh red pesto

METHOD

1 Mix together the potatoes and pesto and serve.

TIP The rest of the pesto can be used on pasta or is very nice mixed
with a few breadcrumbs and used to cover fish before grilling it.

Roast Potatoes

SERVES 4–6 • PREP 15 min • COOKING 40–50 min

INGREDIENTS

1kg potatoes (Maris Piper make
   very good roast potatoes)
100ml olive oil
sprinkling semolina or flour
   (optional – but makes it extra crispy)
salt and pepper

METHOD

1 Preheat the oven to 190°C/375°F/Gas 5.

2 Peel the potatoes and cut each into even-sized pieces
   (a medium potato will cut into four).

3 Bring a pan of salted water to the boil and then boil the
   potatoes for 7 minutes before draining well.

4 Meanwhile, put a roasting tin in the oven with the oil.

5 When the potatoes are ready, either give them a little
   bit of a shake or, using a fork, gently rough up the
   edges.

6 Sprinkle with the semolina or flour and season.

(continued over)

7 Get the hot roasting tin out and carefully tip the potatoes in – they will splash the hot oil!

8 Spread the potatoes out and baste them with the hot oil.

9 Roast the potatoes for 20 minutes, then turn, so they do not stick.

10 Now roast for another 20–30 minutes until they are golden brown and crispy.

Roasted New Potatoes

SERVES 4 • PREP 10 min • COOKING 30 min

INGREDIENTS

500g new potatoes, unpeeled
2 tablespoons oil
4 cloves garlic, unpeeled
1 tablespoon chopped
  fresh rosemary (optional)
salt and black pepper

METHOD

1 Preheat the oven to 180°C/350°F/Gas 4.

2 Cook the potatoes in boiling water for 5 minutes, then
  drain well.

3 Mix together all the ingredients in a bowl, to ensure the
  potatoes are well covered in oil.

4 Tip the contents of the bowl on to a baking tray and
  roast for 30 minutes until the potatoes are well
  browned.

TIP   Other herbs, such as basil or parsley, could be substituted for the
        rosemary.

Wedgy Potatoes

SERVES 2 • PREP 10 min • COOKING 25–30 min

INGREDIENTS

2 large potatoes
2 tablespoons oil
½ teaspoon paprika
1 clove garlic, crushed
salt and pepper

METHOD

1 Preheat the oven to 200°C/400°F/Gas 6.

2 Cut each potato into 8 wedges.

3 Put the wedges in a pan of boiling water and boil for 5 minutes, drain and pat dry.

4 Put all the ingredients into a bowl and stir thoroughly to ensure the potato wedges are covered with oil.

5 Tip on to a roasting tray and cook in the preheated oven for 20–30 minutes until the potatoes are browned and cooked through.

TIP You can make these without pre-boiling, just cook for longer in the oven, but they are much tastier made this way.

These make a change from jacket potatoes and also make a tasty snack when served with a dip and some salad.

Basmati Rice

SERVES 1 • PREP 15 min

INGREDIENTS

50g basmati rice
salt

METHOD

1 Put the rice and a pinch of salt into a saucepan with a lid.

2 Pour on enough boiling water to cover and bring back to the boil.

3 Put the lid on, turn down the heat and simmer for 10 minutes.

4 Drain and then cover with a tea towel or kitchen paper and leave to stand for 2 minutes before serving.

Runner Beans

SERVES 1 • PREP 10–15 min

INGREDIENTS

100g runner beans

METHOD

1 Cut off the ends from the beans.

2 Remove any fibrous strings from the side (most varieties sold now are stringless).

3 Either cut the beans into lengths about 3cm long or, more traditionally but more time consuming, slice them thinly lengthways.

4 Now boil them for 4–8 minutes depending on how thickly you have cut them and how you like them cooked.

5 Try a cooked bean before serving them to see if they're cooked to your liking.

Sweet Potato Baked in Foil

SERVES 1 • PREP 5 min • COOKING 45 min

INGREDIENTS

1 medium sweet potato

METHOD

1 Preheat the oven to 220°C/425°F/Gas 7.

2 Prick the sweet potato all over with a fork.

3 Wrap the potato in foil and bake it in the oven until soft
– about 45 minutes, depending on the size of your
potato.

Egg-fried Rice

SERVES 4 • PREP 5 min

INGREDIENTS

2 tablespoons oil
300g cooked rice
1 egg, lightly beaten
salt and pepper

METHOD

1 Heat the oil in a frying pan or wok and stir-fry the rice.

2 Add the egg and continue to stir until the egg starts to set.

3 Season well and serve.

Chinese Egg-fried Rice

SERVES 4 • PREP 10 min

INGREDIENTS

2 tablespoons oil

200g basmati rice, cooked
and cooled

90g frozen peas

1 bunch of spring onions,
chopped

1 tablespoon soy sauce

1 egg, beaten

METHOD

1 Heat the oil in a frying pan or wok and stir-fry the rice,
peas and spring onions for 2 minutes.

2 Add the soy sauce and egg and continue to stir-fry until
the egg sets.

Pilau Rice

SERVES 4 • PREP 20 min

INGREDIENTS

2 teaspoons oil or butter

1 small onion, chopped

1 stick cinnamon, broken in half

½ teaspoon whole coriander seeds

½ teaspoon whole cardamom pods

½ teaspoon whole cumin seeds

250g basmati rice

500ml vegetable stock,
  made with 1 stock cube
  and boiling water

METHOD

1 Heat the oil or butter in a pan and fry the onion until it is soft and just starting to brown.

2 Add the spices and stir-fry for 30 seconds to 1 minute. This is just to get them to release their flavours, so be careful not to burn them.

3 Add the rice, stir quickly, then add the stock.

4 Bring to the boil, cover tightly and simmer for 10 minutes until the rice has absorbed the stock.

5 Take the pan off the heat but keep it covered and allow it to stand for 3 minutes before stirring the rice and serving it.

Salad Dressing

SERVES 4 • PREP 5 min

INGREDIENTS

4 tablespoons oil
1 tablespoon white wine vinegar
1 teaspoon Dijon mustard
pinch of caster sugar
salt and black pepper

METHOD

1 Put all the ingredients in a screw-top jar and shake well.

LEMON DRESSING

For green salads, mix the juice of half a lemon and
2–3 tablespoons olive oil with a small pinch of sugar and
season it well with salt and pepper.

French Dressing

SERVES 2–3 • PREP 5 min

INGREDIENTS

3 tablespoons olive oil

1 tablespoon tarragon or
white wine vinegar

1 teaspoon mustard powder

1 teaspoon caster sugar

1 teaspoon salt

sprinkling of black pepper

1 clove garlic, crushed
(optional)

METHOD

1 Whisk or shake all the ingredients together.

Carrot Salad

An easy side salad that goes with most dishes, I particularly like this with curries. Sometimes I add a few chopped apricots or raisins to the finished salad.

SERVES 1 • PREP 5 min

INGREDIENTS

1 *large carrot, grated*

FOR THE DRESSING
1 *tablespoon oil*
1 *tablespoon orange juice*
1 *teaspoon wholegrain mustard*
1 *teaspoon white wine vinegar*

METHOD

1 Mix all the dressing ingredients together.

2 Pour the dressing over the grated carrot and serve.

Pan-fried Tomato and Pepper Salad

SERVES 4 • PREP 10 min

INGREDIENTS

2 tablespoons olive oil

2 peppers (yellow and red), deseeded and
  thickly sliced

4 tomatoes, cut into wedges

2 cloves garlic, crushed

1 teaspoon minced chilli

METHOD

1 Heat the oil in a frying pan and fry the peppers until
  they are soft and starting to brown.

2 Add the rest of the ingredients and stir-fry until the
  tomatoes are just beginning to soften.

3 Transfer to a serving dish, scraping all the juices over
  the salad.

Garlic Mushroom Salad

SERVES 4 • PREP 10 min + COOLING TIME

INGREDIENTS

4 tablespoons olive oil
500g button mushrooms, cleaned
6 cloves garlic, crushed
150ml carton sour cream
1 tablespoon chopped chives
salt and black pepper

METHOD

1 Heat the oil in a frying pan and fry the mushrooms and garlic for a few minutes – just enough to soften them.

2 Leave them to cool, then combine with the sour cream and chives.

3 Season and serve.

Mustard-dressed Mixed Salad

SERVES 4 • PREP 5 min

INGREDIENTS

FOR THE SALAD
1 round lettuce
100g mushrooms, sliced
125g packet radishes, sliced
1 carrot, grated
1 heaped tablespoon raisins
1 heaped tablespoon sunflower seeds

FOR THE DRESSING
90ml olive oil
2 tablespoons white wine vinegar
1 clove garlic, crushed
2 teaspoons wholegrain mustard
1 teaspoon Dijon mustard
salt and black pepper

METHOD

1 Combine all the salad ingredients in a large salad bowl.

2 Put all the dressing ingredients in a screw-top jar and shake well, then dress the salad.

Side Salad

SERVES 2 • PREP 5 min

INGREDIENTS

FOR THE SALAD
1 little gem lettuce, shredded
several slices iceberg lettuce
2–3 spring onions, sliced
3–4 radishes, sliced
7cm length of cucumber, sliced

FOR THE DRESSING
2 tablespoons oil
2 teaspoons wine vinegar
1 clove garlic, crushed
pinch of salt
pinch of dried mustard powder

METHOD

1 Place the salad ingredients in a bowl.

2 Mix the dressing ingredients together and pour over the salad just before serving.

Salad with Banana Dressing

SERVES 4 • PREP 10 min

INGREDIENTS

FOR THE SALAD

packet mixed lettuce leaves

*100g white or red cabbage,
  thinly sliced*

1 yellow pepper, chopped

1 punnet of mustard and cress

FOR THE BANANA DRESSING

4 tablespoons oil

1 tablespoon white wine vinegar

1 teaspoon honey

1 banana, chopped finely

salt and pepper

METHOD

1 Place the salad ingredients in a serving bowl.

2 Combine all the dressing ingredients thoroughly and pour over the salad.

3 Mix and serve immediately.

Tabbouleh

SERVES 3–4 • PREP 10 min + STANDING TIME

INGREDIENTS

100g bulgur wheat
juice from 1 large or
  2 small lemons
salt and pepper
4 tablespoons olive oil
2 tablespoons parsley,
  finely chopped
2 tablespoons mint, finely chopped
6 spring onions, sliced
2 tomatoes, peeled and diced

METHOD

1 Soak the bulgur wheat in boiling water for 10 minutes.

2 Rinse and drain, squeezing out as much water as possible.

3 Put the bulgur wheat in a bowl, add the lemon juice and season well.

4 Leave it to stand for 20 minutes.

5 Now add the remaining ingredients and stir well.

Apple Sauce

SERVES 6 • PREP 10–15 min

INGREDIENTS

2 Bramley apples, cored,
   peeled and sliced thickly
2 tablespoons caster sugar
2 tablespoons water

METHOD

1 Put the apples, sugar and water in a small saucepan and
   simmer gently for 5–10 minutes until the apples are soft
   and fluffy. Stir well before serving.

Cheese Sauce

MAKES 350ML • PREP 10 min

INGREDIENTS

300ml milk
25g butter or margarine, softened
25g plain flour
¼ teaspoon mustard powder
50g grated cheese
1 tablespoon cream or milk

METHOD

1 Put the cold milk in a small saucepan and add the butter or margarine, flour and mustard powder.

2 Heat gently, stirring continuously. Keep stirring to keep lumps at bay. I alternate between stirring with a wooden spoon and whisking with a little whisk.

3 The sauce will become quite thick. Turn the heat right down and keep stirring and cooking for 2 minutes.

4 Add the cheese and continue cooking until the cheese has melted.

5 Take the sauce off the heat. Enrich with the cream or slacken with the milk.

6 Use as directed in your chosen recipe.

(continued over)

CREAM SAUCE

Omit the cheese and mustard and add 100ml double cream. Season well with plenty of pepper. Serve with fish or chicken.

MUSHROOM SAUCE

Omit the cheese and mustard. Add 200g sliced fried mushrooms and 2 tablespoons double cream. This is very good with fish or chicken.

Cranberry Sauce with Lime and Ginger

SERVES 6 • PREP 10 min

INGREDIENTS

170g fresh cranberries
3 tablespoons sugar
3 tablespoons maple syrup
3 tablespoons water
1 tablespoon lime juice
1 teaspoon minced ginger

METHOD

1 Put all the ingredients in a saucepan and simmer gently for 5–6 minutes until the sugar has dissolved, the berries have popped and the mixture is just starting to thicken.

TIP   The rest of the cranberries will freeze well for another time.

Fruity Curry Sauce

This is a very easy sauce, which you will probably use time and time again.

SERVES 1–2 • PREP 15 min

INGREDIENTS

1 tablespoon oil
1 onion, diced
1 tablespoon korma paste
1 tablespoon tomato purée
150ml boiling water
1 tablespoon mango chutney
2 tablespoons crème fraîche

METHOD

1 Heat the oil in a frying pan and fry the onion until soft.

2 Stir in the korma paste and tomato purée and cook for 1 minute.

3 Pour in the water and simmer for 3–4 minutes.

4 Now add the rest of the ingredients and the sauce is ready to serve mixed with cooked meats, vegetables, beans or hard-boiled eggs.

Quick Creamy Curry Sauce

SERVES 2 • PREP 10 min

INGREDIENTS

1 tablespoon oil
1 onion, chopped
2 teaspoons curry powder
1 tablespoon mango chutney
150ml carton double cream

METHOD

1 Heat the oil in a pan and fry the onion until it is soft and starting to brown.

2 Mix together the rest of the ingredients, and add the mixture to the pan.

3 Stir until the sauce thickens slightly.

4 Use the sauce to coat cooked vegetables, beans or hard-boiled eggs. Serve with some more mango chutney on the side.

Quick Chilli 'n' Tomato Sauce

SERVES 1 • PREP 5 min

INGREDIENTS

1 tablespoon chilli relish
1 tablespoon tomato purée
1 tablespoon boiling water

METHOD

1 Mix all the ingredients together and use as a sauce for savoury dishes.

Salsa

Although you can now buy many varieties of salsa in the shops – and some of them are very good – I still like to make my own. You can alter the heat of your salsa by varying the amount of chilli you use.

SERVES 4–6 • PREP 15 min

INGREDIENTS

2 tablespoons oil
½ green pepper, finely chopped
1 small onion, finely chopped
2 cloves garlic, crushed
sprinkling of chilli powder
230g can chopped tomatoes
1 tablespoon tomato purée

METHOD

1 Heat 1 tablespoon of the oil in a pan and fry the pepper and onion for 5 minutes.

2 Add the garlic, chilli powder and tomatoes, and simmer gently for 5 minutes.

3 Finally, add the rest of the oil and the tomato purée, stir and leave the salsa to cool.

Yorkshire Puddings

SERVES 6 • PREP 10 min • COOKING 15–20 min

INGREDIENTS

oil for cooking
100g plain flour
pinch of salt
2 eggs, beaten
100ml each of milk and water, mixed together

METHOD

1 Preheat the oven to 220°C/425°F/Gas 7.

2 Put some oil in each of the holes of a twelve-hole bun tin.

3 Put the tin in the oven to heat up.

4 Put the flour and salt in a mixing bowl.

5 Make a well in the middle and pour in the eggs and half of the milk mixture.

6 Mix the flour into the liquid and mix until you have a thick batter.

7 Gradually beat in the rest of the milk. Divide the mixture among the bun holes and return the tin to the oven.

8 Cook for 15–20 minutes or until the puddings are well risen and browned.

TIP If cooking these with a roast, put the oil in the tin to heat up for 15 minutes before the roast is due to come out. When the roast comes out, turn the heat up to full power and then get these cooking while the meat rests and is then carved.

---

6 Sweet Things

Everyone likes a treat now and again. Although students do not often bother with desserts, occasionally you will want to indulge yourself. These recipes are very easy to make – in fact, I like to think they are foolproof, although I know there are those who somehow will manage to go astray . . . Everyone has a disaster some time. A friend recently reminded me of the occasion when I made a cake that came out flat as a pancake – I had forgotten to put in the flour! And not so long ago we waited rather a long time for a cake to cook, as someone (who shall remain nameless) hadn't turned the oven on . . .

I fondly remember the pancake parties that one of our friends used to give. He was an absolute ace at pancakes and provided lots of scrummy fillings. As long as we kept him supplied with drinks, he kept us supplied with pancakes. We helped ourselves as the pancakes arrived – and just kept going until we were in danger of bursting!

THE CHOICES:

PUDDINGS

Pancakes

Baked Apples Stuffed with Mincemeat

Danish Apple Pudding

Microwave Apple Cinnamon Pudding

Rhubarb Crumble

Apple and Blackberry Pie

Stewed Fruit

Lychees and Mangoes

Eton Mess

Poached Pears in Cider

Ricotta with Honey and Pine Nuts

Trifle

Chocolate Tiramisu

Mummy's Baked Custard

Rice Pudding

Greek Honey-nut Pie

Banoffee Pie

Chocomallow Pie

Brown Bread Ice Cream

Ice Cream with Chocolate Fudge Sauce

Microwave Snickers Sauce (for Ice Cream)

Butterscotch Sauce (for Ice Cream)

TEA-TIME TREATS

Brownies

Chocolate Chip Cookies

Cascake

Cinnamon Rock Buns

Peanut Crumblies

Flapjacks

Chocolate Squares

Fairy Cakes

Chocolate Rice Crispy Cakes

Chocolate Mini Muffins

Gingerbread Loaf

Crispy Marshmallow Squares

Easy Fruit Cake

Passion Cake

Lemon Drizzle Cake

PUDDINGS

Pancakes

SERVES 2–3 • PREP 10 min • COOKING 2 min EACH PANCAKE

INGREDIENTS

100g plain flour
pinch of salt
1 egg, beaten
250ml milk
oil or butter for frying
sugar to serve
lemon to serve

METHOD

1 Sift the flour and salt into a bowl.

2 Make a well in the middle and pour the egg and half the milk into it.

3 Beat together well, gradually adding more milk until you have a smooth thin batter.

4 Heat a little oil or butter in a small frying pan and ladle in just enough pancake mixture to cover the bottom of the pan.

5 Cook until the bottom of the pancake starts to brown (lift the pancake at the edge to check).

6 Flip(!) the pancake over and cook the other side for 1 minute.

7 Slide the pancake on to a serving plate and sprinkle with sugar and a squeeze of lemon.

Baked Apples Stuffed with Mincemeat

SERVES 4 • PREP 5 min • COOKING 45–60 min

INGREDIENTS

4 *large Bramley apples, cored*
3 *tablespoons mincemeat (sweet!)*
2 *tablespoons water*

METHOD

1 Preheat the oven to 180°C/350°F/Gas 4.

2 Score around the middle of the apples and put them in a baking dish.

3 Fill each apple cavity with the mincemeat.

4 Pour the water into the baking dish and cook in the preheated oven for 45–60 minutes until the apples are soft.

TIP My mother makes baked apples as above but uses a mixture of sultanas, butter and sugar instead of mincemeat to stuff the apples.

Danish Apple Pudding

SERVES 4 • PREP 20 min + COOLING TIME

INGREDIENTS

1kg Bramley apples,
  peeled and diced
75g butter
honey, golden syrup or sugar,
  to taste
150g fresh wholemeal
  breadcrumbs
50g soft dark brown sugar

METHOD

1 Cook the apples in a pan with 25g of the butter until they are very soft (this takes about 6–8 minutes).

2 In the pan, mash the apples into a purée and sweeten to taste. Leave to cool.

3 Meanwhile, heat the remaining butter and fry the breadcrumbs with the brown sugar until they start to crisp, then leave them to cool.

4 When both the apple purée and crumbs are cold, layer them into 4 small serving bowls, alternating layers of fruit with crumbs, finishing with a layer of crumbs.

Microwave Apple Cinnamon Pudding

SERVES 1 • PREP 10 min + STANDING TIME

INGREDIENTS

1 eating apple, cored,
  peeled and sliced
1 teaspoon water
knob of butter
2 tablespoons soft brown
  sugar
2 tablespoons flour
sprinkling of cinnamon

METHOD

1 Put the apple and water in a microwaveable dish.

2 Using your fingertips, rub together the butter, sugar and flour. Keep rubbing until you have a breadcrumb-like mixture.

3 Sprinkle with cinnamon and mix it in.

4 Sprinkle the mixture over the apple.

5 Cover and cook for 3 minutes until the topping is cooked and the apple is tender.

6 Leave it to stand for 5 minutes.

Rhubarb Crumble

SERVES 4 • PREP 10 min • COOKING 40–50 min + STANDING TIME

INGREDIENTS

500g rhubarb
2–3 tablespoons caster sugar
1 teaspoon mixed spice
juice and grated peel of
   1 large orange

FOR THE CRUMBLE

50g butter
125g flour
3 tablespoons caster sugar

METHOD

1 Preheat the oven to 180°C/350°F/Gas 4.

2 Trim the ends off the rhubarb. Cut the rhubarb into 3cm pieces.

3 Place the rhubarb, sugar, mixed spice, orange juice and peel in an ovenproof dish.

4 Rub together the crumble ingredients until you have a mixture resembling breadcrumbs and spoon this over the rhubarb.

(continued over)

5 Cook, uncovered, in the preheated oven for 35–40 minutes or until it is lightly browned and juices are starting to bubble up.

6 Leave it to stand for 5–10 minutes before serving.

TIP   This is a favourite for a Sunday lunch dessert. Serve with cream, crème fraîche or custard. The crumble topping can be used to cover other seasonal fruit. e.g. for an apple crumble, which is made exactly the same way but substitute Bramley apples for the rhubarb and orange.

Apple and Blackberry Pie

SERVES 4–6 • PREP 15 min • COOKING 30 min

INGREDIENTS

500g Bramley cooking apples,
  peeled, cored and cut into large chunks
225g fresh blackberries
2 heaped tablespoons caster sugar
200–225g frozen shortcrust
  pastry sheet, defrosted
1 egg white, beaten

METHOD

1 Preheat the oven to 200°C/400°F/Gas 6.

2 In a small ovenproof dish, pile the apples and blackberries, and sprinkle in half the sugar.

3 Place the pastry sheet over the top and mould it to the sides of the dish.

4 Brush the top with the egg white and then sprinkle with the remaining sugar.

5 Cut a small hole in the middle of the pastry so that steam can escape during cooking.

6 Cook in the preheated oven for 30 minutes.

APPLE PIE

If blackberries are not in season, substitute an equal amount of extra apple for the blackberries plus maybe a few cloves or a sprinkling of cinnamon.

Stewed Fruit

SERVES 4 • PREP 10–15 min

INGREDIENTS

450g rhubarb, gooseberries
  or blackberries, washed
2 tablespoons sugar
2 tablespoons water

METHOD

1 Choose your fruit and prepare it accordingly. For
   rhubarb, trim off both ends and then cut the sticks into
   short lengths. For gooseberries, you need to trim off
   both ends. Blackberries need no preparation.

2 Put all ingredients in a pan and cook for 10–15 minutes
   until the fruit is soft.

TIP Serve with custard or ice cream. As a contrast to the soft fruit, it is
nice to serve some crunchy biscuits also.

Lychees and Mangoes

SERVES 4 • PREP 5 min

INGREDIENTS

425g can lychees
410g can mangoes

METHOD

1 Drain both cans, reserving 4 tablespoons syrup from the can of mangoes.

2 Divide the fruit among 4 serving bowls and spoon some of the reserved juice over each.

3 Chill until you are ready to serve.

Eton Mess

SERVES 4–6 • PREP 20 min

INGREDIENTS

450g strawberries, sliced

1 tablespoon caster sugar

4–6 meringue nests, broken

300ml whipping cream,
   whipped until starting to thicken

METHOD

1 Mix together the strawberries and sugar and leave them to chill for 1 hour to allow the strawberry juices to flow.

2 When you are ready to make the pudding, mix all the ingredients together and pile them into a huge bowl to serve.

TIP Make this when strawberries are plentiful, not in the middle of winter when only imported expensive ones are available.

Poached Pears in Cider

SERVES 2 • PREP 15 min • COOKING 20–30 min

INGREDIENTS

660ml medium-dry cider
125g caster sugar
1 cinnamon stick, broken in half
1 vanilla pod (optional)
2 hard well-shaped pears
1 unwaxed lemon, thinly sliced

METHOD

1   In a saucepan that allows you to place your pears side by side lengthways, bring half the cider to the boil, add the sugar and the cinnamon stick pieces.

2   Slice halfway into your vanilla pod (if using) and scrape some of the seeds into the cider, then put the pod itself in.

3   Simmer very gently while you prepare the pears.

4   Carefully peel off the skin (a vegetable peeler is very handy here), leaving the stem on.

5   Now place the pears in the simmering cider and cover with slices of lemon. Add as much more cider as is needed to just cover the pears. Simmer very gently for 20–30 minutes.

6   Start testing for softness after 20 minutes. You do want them to be soft but not with a 'pappy' texture.

(continued over)

7 When the pears are done, leave them to cool in the syrup.

8 Transfer the pears to a serving bowl with a slotted spoon. Now remove the cinnamon stick, vanilla pod and lemon slices.

9 Bring the syrup to the boil and reduce it by half or until you have a thicker syrup.

10 Cool and pour a little of the syrup over the pears.

TIP If you have a freezer, you can freeze the remainder of the syrup and when serving your pears scrape a few slithers of frozen syrup over them.

Ricotta with Honey and Pine Nuts

SERVES 2 • PREP 5 min

INGREDIENTS

2 tablespoons runny honey
250g tub ricotta cheese
1 tablespoon pine nuts

METHOD

1 Mix 2 teaspoons of the honey with the cheese and then divide the cheese between two bowls.

2 Drizzle the remaining honey over the ricotta and sprinkle with the nuts.

Trifle

SERVES 6–8 • PREP 20 min

INGREDIENTS

FOR THE TRIFLE

70g packet instant custard mix
8 trifle sponges
2 tablespoons raspberry jam
125ml sherry or orange juice
20 ratafia biscuits, crushed
400g can mango slices, drained
1 banana, sliced

FOR DECORATION

250ml carton whipping cream
whole ratafia biscuits
fresh raspberries or hundreds
  and thousands and/or silver
  dragées or chopped roasted nuts

METHOD

1 Make up the instant custard as directed on the packet. Cool it slightly.

2 Split the trifle sponges and sandwich them together with the jam. Arrange them in a serving bowl and spoon in the sherry or orange juice. Cover with the crushed ratafia biscuits.

3 Add the mango and banana to the trifle and cover with custard. Chill.

4 Whip the cream, spoon it over the cold trifle. Arrange the biscuits and your chosen decoration on top.

TIP   This is really where you can let your imagination go wild. Basically, you can use most types of cake instead of the trifle sponges, you can substitute many different fruits, fresh or canned, use a carton of custard, mix the custard with cream or mascarpone, or use sweet wine, rum or a liqueur instead of sherry. Make up your own version!

Chocolate Tiramisu

SERVES 4–6 • PREP 15 min

INGREDIENTS

250g mascarpone cheese
2 egg yolks, beaten
2 tablespoons caster sugar
1 teaspoon vanilla essence
200ml double-strength black coffee
miniature brandy or amaretto
box of sponge fingers
2 chocolate Flakes, crumbled

METHOD

1   Beat together the mascarpone cheese, egg yolks, sugar and vanilla essence.

2   Mix together the coffee and brandy or amaretto.

3   Dip half the sponge fingers into the coffee mixture and arrange them in a serving dish.

4   Cover with half the mascarpone mixture and half the chocolate Flake.

5   Dip the remaining fingers in the coffee and arrange in another layer on top.

6   Cover with the rest of the mascarpone mixture and sprinkle the rest of the chocolate over it.

7   Chill before serving.

Mummy's Baked Custard

You can improve the texture of your custard by placing the custard dish in a roasting tin with enough boiling water to come halfway up the dish. Then bake as below.

SERVES 2–3 • PREP 5 min • COOKING 40–50 min

INGREDIENTS

2 whole eggs and 1 yolk
1 tablespoon sugar
several drops of vanilla essence
250ml milk
grated nutmeg (optional)
knob of butter

METHOD

1 Preheat the oven to 150°C/300°F/Gas 2.

2 Beat together the eggs, yolk, sugar and vanilla essence.

3 Put the milk into a small saucepan and bring it to boiling point.

4 Remove the milk from the heat immediately, pour it on to the egg and sugar mixture and stir well.

5 Pour into a greased pie dish or small casserole dish and sprinkle with grated nutmeg (if using).

6 Put a little knob of butter on top and bake in the preheated oven for 40–50 minutes until the custard has set and a skin has formed.

Rice Pudding

SERVES 2–3 • PREP 5 min • COOKING 120 min

INGREDIENTS

2 tablespoons pudding rice
1 tablespoon sugar
500ml milk
knob of butter
grated nutmeg (optional)

METHOD

1 Preheat the oven to 150°C/300°F/Gas 2.

2 Put the rice, sugar and milk in a greased pie dish or small casserole dish.

3 Top with little pieces of butter and sprinkle with grated nutmeg (if using).

4 Bake in the preheated oven for about 2 hours, until the rice has absorbed the milk and a skin has formed.

Greek Honey-nut Pie

This is an incredibly rich recipe – but utterly delicious! You
must serve it in small portions and only on special occasions,
as I hate to think what it does to the waistline! Sweet pastry
shells can be bought in most large supermarkets and are very
good.

SERVES 6–8 • PREP 10 min • COOKING 25–30 min

INGREDIENTS

3 tablespoons caster sugar

3 tablespoons Greek honey

3 tablespoons double cream

75g butter, chopped

*150g mixed nuts, such as pecans
    and hazelnuts, chopped*

190g sweet pastry shell

METHOD

1   Preheat the oven to 190°C/375°F/Gas 5.

2   In a small pan, dissolve the sugar in the honey, stirring
    over a gentle heat, then boil for 3 minutes.

3   Add the cream and butter and beat well.

4   Stir in the nuts and pour the mixture into the pastry
    shell.

5   Level the top and bake in the preheated oven for
    25–30 minutes.

Banoffee Pie

This is such an easy dessert to make now – and it will make you very popular with your friends!

SERVES 6 • PREP 10 min + CHILLING TIME

INGREDIENTS

195g sweet pastry shell

2 large or 3 small ripe bananas, mashed

397g can Carnation caramel

300ml whipping cream

25g Flake, crumbled, or a small piece (5g) dark chocolate, grated

METHOD

1 Cover the base of the pastry shell with the mashed banana.

2 Spoon the caramel carefully over the banana. Put the pie into the fridge while you whip the cream.

3 Whip the cream so that it is stiff enough to hold its shape but not so thick that it won't spread. (This takes me about 5 minutes with a hand-held whisk.)

4 Remove the pie from the fridge and spoon the cream over it so that it covers the caramel filling.

5 Sprinkle over the chocolate topping.

6 Chill for at least 1 hour before serving.

TIP If you really don't want to be bothered with whipping the cream, buy an aerosol of whipping cream and cover the caramel with this just before serving. (It's not quite as good, but it is an acceptable substitute.)

Chocomallow Pie

This is based on that old favourite, Mississippi mud pie.

SERVES 8 • PREP 20–25 min + CHILLING TIME

INGREDIENTS

195g sweet pastry shell

300ml double cream

100g dark chocolate,
  broken into small pieces

100g mini marshmallows

25g Flake, crumbled, or a
  small piece (5g) dark chocolate,
  grated as topping

METHOD

1 Place the pastry shell on your serving plate.

2 Put half the cream, plus the chocolate and the mini marshmallows in a small saucepan and gently heat while stirring until you have a smooth mixture. (This takes about 2–3 minutes.)

3 Remove from the heat and keep beating and lifting the spoon out of the pan and letting the mixture drop back into the pan – this makes for a very smooth mixture and helps it to cool.

4 Then pour about ⅔ of the mixture into the pastry shell and smooth so that it covers the bottom.

5 Leave the mixtures to cool while you beat the remaining cream into a soft set – thick enough to hold its shape but still soft enough to spread.

6 When the saucepan mixture is cold, spoon some into the cream and mix through, repeating until all the chocolate mixture is incorporated. Don't mix it in thoroughly, as a marbled effect is what we are after.

7 Spoon this chocolate cream on to the pie and spread it all over.

8 Sprinkle with the crumbled or grated chocolate.

9 Chill for at least 1 hour.

Brown Bread Ice Cream

This is utterly delectable. I don't know if you should risk making this if you live in hall, as it must be left in the freezer compartment of the refrigerator and in a communal kitchen this could be risky. It would be tragic to discover that someone else had been unable to resist your delicious dessert!

SERVES 4 • PREP 20 min + FREEZING TIME

INGREDIENTS

2 large slices wholemeal bread,
  crumbed
6 tablespoons soft brown sugar
140ml carton whipping cream
300g Greek yogurt

METHOD

1 Preheat the oven to 200°C/400°F/Gas 6.

2 Cover a baking tray with foil. Mix together the breadcrumbs and sugar and spread this over the covered baking tray.

3 Bake in the preheated oven for 10 minutes.

4 Whip the cream until it forms soft peaks, then stir in the yogurt.

5 Mix in the caramelised breadcrumbs and put it into a freezer-proof container.

6 Freeze for 4 hours, then transfer the ice cream to the fridge for 30 minutes before serving.

Ice Cream with Chocolate Fudge Sauce

This is utterly delicious and very popular in our house.

SERVES 4 • PREP 10 min

INGREDIENTS

65g Mars bar, chopped
1 tablespoon butter
1 tablespoon soft brown sugar
1 tablespoon boiling water
500ml vanilla ice cream

METHOD

1 Place a heatproof bowl over a small saucepan of boiling water. Don't let the bowl touch the water.

2 Put the Mars bar, butter and sugar in the bowl to melt.

3 Then beat in the water.

4 When the sauce is smooth, pour it over the ice cream and serve.

Microwave Snickers Sauce (for Ice Cream)

SERVES 2 • PREP 5 min

INGREDIENTS

1 Snickers bar, chopped
2 tablespoons milk

METHOD

1 Put the Snickers bar and milk into a microwaveable dish.

2 Cover and cook for 45 seconds, remove the top carefully (beware of hot steam), stir, re-cover and cook for another 45 seconds.

3 As before, be very careful when removing the top. Stir and let stand for a few minutes before serving, but serve hot over cold ice cream.

Butterscotch Sauce (for Ice Cream)

SERVES 4 • PREP 10 min

INGREDIENTS

150ml tub double cream
½ teaspoon vanilla extract
75g butter
100g soft dark brown sugar

METHOD

1 Put all the ingredients in a medium saucepan and gently heat until you have a smooth sauce.

2 Now bring the sauce to the boil and cook for a few minutes to thicken it.

3 Serve hot.

TEA-TIME TREATS

Brownies

MAKES 16 • PREP 15 min • COOKING 30 min

INGREDIENTS

250g butter
200g chocolate
50g cocoa powder
100g self-raising flour
250g sugar
3 eggs, beaten
100g walnut pieces

METHOD

1 Preheat the oven to 180°C/350°F/Gas 4.

2 Melt together the butter and chocolate in a bowl over a pan of simmering water.

3 When smooth, leave it to cool.

4 Mix together the flour and sugar and then beat in the eggs.

5 Mix in the chocolate and butter and then the walnuts.

6 Put into a lined 24 x 24cm tin.

7 Bake for 30 minutes.

8 Leave to cool. The brownies will still be soft in the centre but will firm up a little while cooling.

Chocolate Chip Cookies

MAKES 12 • PREP 15 min • COOKING 8–10 min

INGREDIENTS

100g butter, softened
125g caster sugar
1 egg, beaten
1 teaspoon vanilla extract (optional)
150g self-raising flour
100g chocolate chips

METHOD

1 Preheat the oven to 190°C/375°F/Gas 5.

2 Beat together the butter and sugar, then beat in the egg and the vanilla extract (if using).

3 Beat in the flour.

4 When thoroughly mixed, add the chocolate chips.

5 Put some greaseproof paper over 2 baking trays.

6 Put 6 mounds of your cookie mixture on each sheet, leaving as much space as possible between them.

7 Bake in the preheated oven for 8–10 minutes until the cookies are a light brown colour.

8 Take them out of the oven and leave them for a few minutes to harden.

DOUBLE CHOCOLATE CHIP COOKIES

Add 2 tablespoons cocoa powder to the mixture and just use 125g flour.

Cascake

This is my version of chocolate fudge cake and makes an excellent birthday treat for some lucky person. I originally used to make the topping with a more traditional mix of buttercream and chocolate Flake but have found it simpler to use melted Mars bars instead.

SERVES 8–12 • PREP 25 min • COOKING 25–30 min + COOLING TIME

INGREDIENTS

FOR THE CAKE

125g soft margarine or butter

125g soft brown sugar

2 eggs, beaten

1 tablespoon cocoa powder
made up to 125g with
self-raising flour

FOR THE ICING

3 x 65g Mars bars

25g butter

50g soft brown sugar

METHOD

1 Preheat the oven to 190°C/375°F/Gas 5.

2 Grease an 18cm cake tin or line it with greaseproof paper.

(continued over)

3 Beat together the cake ingredients and spoon the mixture into the cake tin. Level the surface.

4 Bake in the preheated oven for 25–30 minutes until the cake is well risen and brown.

5 When the cake is cooked, leave it to cool before decorating it.

6 Chop 2 Mars bars and slice the third (into about 16 thin slices).

7 In a heatproof bowl placed over simmering water, melt the chopped Mars bars and butter. Don't let the water touch the bottom of the bowl. Do this slowly. When melted, beat in the sugar and spread this mixture over the cake. Decorate with the slices of Mars bar, and leave the icing to harden in the refrigerator.

Cinnamon Rock Buns

MAKES 6 • PREP 10 min • COOKING 20 min

INGREDIENTS

200g self-raising flour
1 teaspoon ground cinnamon
100g butter or margarine
100g demerara sugar,
  plus 1 tablespoon
1 egg, beaten
2 tablespoons milk

METHOD

1 Preheat the oven to 200°C/400°F/Gas 6.

2 Rub together the flour, cinnamon, butter or margarine and 100g sugar until they resemble breadcrumbs.

3 Stir in the egg and milk.

4 Drop 6 spoonfuls of the mixture on to a non-stick baking tray (or one covered with greaseproof paper) and sprinkle with the remaining tablespoon of demerara sugar.

5 Bake in the preheated oven for 20 minutes until golden brown.

6 These buns are best served while still warm.

Peanut Crumblies

MAKES 16 BISCUITS • PREP 15–20 min

INGREDIENTS

100g butter, softened
100g crunchy peanut butter
100g soft brown sugar
150g plain flour
1–2 teaspoons water

METHOD

1 Preheat the oven to 190°C/375°F/Gas 5.

2 Cream together the butters and sugar until fluffy.

3 Stir in the flour and mix to a dough using the water to help.

4 Divide into 16, roll into little balls and place these on 2 non-stick baking trays.

5 Using a dampened fork, flatten each ball into a biscuit, but make sure they don't stick to the trays.

6 Bake in the preheated oven for 15–20 minutes.

7 Leave on the trays for 10 minutes before very carefully transferring them to a wire rack to cool.

Flapjacks

MAKES 12 • PREP 10 min • COOKING 20 min

INGREDIENTS

125g soft butter or margarine
125g soft brown sugar
1 tablespoon golden syrup
175g oats

METHOD

1 Preheat the oven to 190°C/375°F/Gas 5.

2 Melt the butter or margarine, sugar and syrup together.

3 Stir in the oats.

4 Grease a 28 x 18cm tin and spoon the mixture into it.

5 Press the mixture into the base of the tin and level it.

6 Bake in the preheated oven for about 20 minutes.

7 Mark into portions but leave in the tin to cool.

8 When cold, cut out the individual flapjacks.

MUESLI FLAPJACKS

Use the above recipe but add an extra tablespoon of golden syrup, reduce the amount of oats to 100g and add 100g muesli.

CHOCOLATE FLAPJACKS

Use the above recipe but add a tablespoon of cocoa when you melt the ingredients together.

Chocolate Squares

MAKES 24 • PREP 15 min

INGREDIENTS

200g plain chocolate
75g margarine or butter
3 tablespoons runny honey
300g digestive or ginger biscuits,
 roughly crushed
24 Maltesers

METHOD

1 Melt the chocolate, margarine or butter and honey.

2 Stir in the crushed biscuits and mix thoroughly.

3 Turn into a greased and lined baking tin, about
 28 x 18cm. Level the mixture.

4 Spacing the Maltesers equally apart, and making 4 lines
 of 6 Maltesers, push them down into the mixture.

5 Leave to set and then cut into squares with a Malteser
 in the middle of each square.

Fairy Cakes

MAKES 12 • PREP 15 min • COOKING 15 min

INGREDIENTS

FOR THE SPONGE
100g soft butter or margarine
100g caster sugar
100g self-raising flour
2 eggs, beaten

FOR THE BUTTERCREAM
25g butter, softened
50g icing sugar
several drops of vanilla essence
1–2 teaspoons milk

METHOD

1 Preheat the oven to 190°C/375°F/Gas 5.

2 Beat all the cake ingredients together.

3 Spread out 12 paper cake cases on a baking tray and divide the mixture among them.

4 Bake in the preheated oven for about 15 minutes until the cakes are golden brown and feel 'springy' when touched.

5 Leave on a wire rack to cool.

6 Make the buttercream by beating the butter, sugar and vanilla essence together, adding just enough milk to form a smooth cream. Put some buttercream on each cake.

Chocolate Rice Crispy Cakes

MAKES 16–20 • PREP 10 min

INGREDIENTS

150g plain or milk chocolate
100g puffed Rice Crispies

METHOD

1 Break up the chocolate and place it in a glass bowl.

2 Gently melt the chocolate either over a saucepan of boiling water or in the microwave – but do it gently or the chocolate will seize up and have a burnt flavour.

3 Mix with the crispies and divide the mixture into some paper cups.

4 Leave it to set.

Chocolate Mini Muffins

MAKES 12 • PREP 10 min • COOKING 10–12 min

INGREDIENTS

1 medium egg, beaten
60ml milk
25g butter, melted
75g plain flour
1 tablespoon cocoa powder
1 teaspoon baking powder
25g caster sugar
50g chocolate buttons,
   roughly broken

METHOD

1 Preheat the oven to 190°C/375°F/Gas 5.

2 Lightly mix the egg, milk and butter together.

3 Sieve in the flour, cocoa powder and baking powder.

4 Add the rest of the ingredients and lightly mix.

5 You will have a lumpy mixture. This is what you want –
do not over-mix it.

6 Divide the mixture among 12 mini muffin cases and
bake in the preheated oven for 10–12 minutes until the
muffins have risen.

7 Transfer them in their cases to a cooling rack.

Gingerbread Loaf

MAKES 2 x 1lb LOAVES • PREP 15 min • COOKING 50–60 min

INGREDIENTS

100g butter

100g golden syrup
  (4 scant tablespoons)

100g treacle (4 scant tablespoons)

100g soft brown sugar
  (4 heaped tablespoons)

225g self-raising flour
  (12 rounded tablespoons)

1 teaspoon ground ginger
  (2 if you like it really spicy)

1 teaspoon mixed spice

½ teaspoon bicarbonate of soda

2 eggs, beaten

125ml milk

50–60g stem ginger (2 pieces),
  well drained and finely
  chopped (optional)

METHOD

1 Preheat the oven to 170°C/325°F/Gas 3.

2 Put the butter, syrup, treacle and sugar into a saucepan and cook gently until the butter has melted and the sugar has dissolved.

3 Mix the dry ingredients together. Then mix together the eggs and milk.

4 Finally, mix all the ingredients together with the chopped stem ginger (if using).

5 Put in 2 lined 400g (13 x 7.5 x 7.5cm) loaf tins.

6 Bake in the preheated oven for 50–60 minutes or until an inserted skewer comes out clean.

7 Transfer to a cooling rack.

8 When cool, wrap in foil and it will become lovely and sticky.

Crispy Marshmallow Squares

**MAKES 8–9 PIECES DEPENDING ON THE TIN USED •
PREP 10 min**

INGREDIENTS

100g white chocolate

75g butter

75g golden syrup

100g puffed rice

50g semi-dried, ready-to-eat apricots,
 chopped

25g mini marshmallows

METHOD

1 Melt together the chocolate, butter and syrup in a large
 bowl over a saucepan of boiling water.

2 When smooth, take the bowl off the heat and add the
 rest of the ingredients.

3 Stir well and spoon the mixture into a 20cm baking tin,
 greased and lined with greaseproof paper.

4 Level the top, pressing down quite hard to compact it.
 Leave it to set.

5 Cut into pieces with a sharp knife.

Easy Fruit Cake

This is very easy to make and tastes really good. It keeps well in a cake tin and is a great addition to packed lunches. Make sure that the butter or margarine is nice and soft or it will take you forever to cream the mixture.

MAKES 12 PORTIONS • PREP 15 min • COOKING 50–60 min + STANDING TIME

INGREDIENTS

150g soft butter or margarine
150g muscovado sugar
3 eggs, beaten
200g self-raising wholemeal flour
1 teaspoon ground cinnamon
250g luxury dried fruit mix
100g glacé cherries, chopped

METHOD

1 Preheat the oven to 170°C/325°F/Gas 3.

2 Beat together the butter or margarine and sugar until creamy.

3 Gently beat in the eggs, a little at a time, adding a little flour with the egg to stop the mixture from curdling.

4 Then fold in the remaining flour, cinnamon, fruit mix and cherries.

(continued over)

5 Line an 18cm-deep cake tin with baking parchment or greaseproof paper, spoon the mixture into the tin and level it.

6 Cook in the preheated oven for 50–60 minutes until the cake has risen and is brown and firm to the touch.

7 Leave it in the tin for 20 minutes, then transfer it to a wire rack, peel off the baking parchment or greaseproof paper and leave it to cool.

8 Top with the glacé cherries.

Passion Cake

SERVES 8–12 • PREP 15 min • COOKING 90 min

INGREDIENTS

FOR THE SPONGE

200g soft butter or margarine
200g soft brown sugar
4 eggs, beaten
200g wholemeal self-raising flour
1 teaspoon baking powder
300g carrots, peeled and grated
grated rind of 1 lemon and
   1 tablespoon of the juice
100g chopped walnuts

FOR THE ICING

75g cream cheese
50g icing sugar
grated rind and juice of 1 orange

METHOD

1 Preheat the oven to 180°C/350°F/Gas 4.

2 Beat together the butter or margarine, sugar, eggs, flour, baking powder, carrots, lemon rind and juice and walnuts.

3 Put the mixture in a greased and lined 20cm-deep cake tin.

(continued over)

4 Bake in the preheated oven for about 90 minutes until it is well risen and golden brown.

5 Leave the cake to cool, while you prepare the icing. Beat together the cream cheese and icing sugar and use just enough orange juice to achieve a creamy consistency.

6 Cover the top of the cake with the icing and sprinkle the orange rind over it.

Lemon Drizzle Cake

SERVES 6 • PREP 15 min • COOKING 40 min

INGREDIENTS

100g soft margarine
200g caster sugar
2 eggs, beaten
100g self-raising flour
rind and juice of 1 lemon

METHOD

1 Preheat the oven to 180°C/350°F/Gas 4.

2 Beat the margarine with half the sugar.

3 Beat in the eggs and then gently stir in the flour and the lemon rind.

4 Put in a greased and lined 20cm-deep cake tin and bake in the preheated oven for 40 minutes.

5 Remove the cake to a cooling tray.

6 Mix the remaining sugar with the lemon juice and spoon over the top of the cake. As the cake cools, this will form a sugar crust.

7 Easy Entertaining Ideas
including lots of cocktails and mocktails

Although entertaining is not an aspect of cooking that people generally consider when they think of student cooking, it is something that many students find very enjoyable. You don't have to be a gourmet chef to be able to cook dinner parties. With tried and tested recipes even those who have little experience can entertain their friends. Just to get you started, I have put together some ideas for menus to use when making a meal for friends. The ones that I have chosen are varied and mirror meals that students would generally enjoy in restaurants – but at a fraction of the cost.

Organisation is the key to happy entertaining – check and double-check! Be particularly wary of assuming that you have an ingredient in your store cupboard only to discover at the last minute that what you actually have is a nearly empty container.

I have arranged this chapter to make it as easy as possible for you. For each menu I have worked out a shopping list and a time plan. Just remember: a) if you are providing the drinks, you need to add these to your shopping list (ditto coffee, tea and milk if you are serving them); b) the time plan is the preparation time *after* you have got everything ready – that is, chopped the vegetables, precooked any items, etc. Only you can estimate how long that will take you.

Occasionally you may want to get together with a group of friends to cook a meal and have a few drinks. This might be for a specific reason, i.e. a birthday celebration or the end of term or just because the sun is shining and it feels like a good idea.

Over many years I have come to the conclusion that the easiest way of entertaining large numbers is to have most of the dishes already prepared, so I rely increasingly on salads that can be made up and will sit happily for a time while other last-minute preparations are in hand. For these salads I have drawn on inspiration from many different cultures. I used to theme meals, but nowadays just mix and match as I feel like it.

Some points to bear in mind:

CATERING FOR UP TO 8

Serve 1 mixed salad and 1 main dish.

CATERING FOR 9–12

Serve 2 salads and 1 main dish.

CATERING FOR 13–16

Serve 2 salads and 2 main courses.

Serve a selection of dips and tortilla chips, a simple green leaf salad with dressing or mayonnaise, and some French sticks or garlic bread alongside these dishes. As a treat, you could provide a pudding. There are many to choose from in the shops, or you could make the very simple Eton Mess (page 358), which is a mixture of whipped cream, strawberries and broken meringues. Just remember to multiply the recipe for the number of people you are catering for.

Some people like to get together and decide on a sum that will cover the food and drink as well, or you can just share the cost of the cooking and get everyone to bring their own favourite drink (this works well if you have a mixture of heavy drinkers and teetotallers).

On the subject of drink, it's amazing how popular cocktails are with students. However, they can be very expensive when bought in restaurants and clubs. If you have friends with similar tastes in drinks, a pleasant evening can be had by pooling together to buy the ingredients and having a night in. Cocktail parties are also very popular, especially when celebrating a birthday or other special event.

While we were at university, my friend Lucy celebrated her 21st birthday with a cocktail party and it went down very well. It is important to have enough helpers (who know what they are doing) at these events. We decided on what cocktails were going to be on offer and drew large pictures of these to hang on the walls – this meant that people knew what they were ordering and the helpers knew what to put in them! It is also important to have plenty of ice and glasses on hand as people usually have a new glass when they have a different cocktail.

I have given a range of non-alcoholic drinks here as well, as contrary to belief not all students like to imbibe huge quantities of alcohol (no, honestly!).

THE CHOICES:

COCKTAILS

Appletini

B-52

Between-the-sheets

Black Russian

Brandy Alexander

Caipirinha

Cosmopolitan

FBI

Harvey Wallbanger

Head Honcho

June Bug

Kamikaze

Long Island Iced Tea

Lynchburg Lemonade

Mai Tai

Margarita

Martini

Melon Daiquiri

Mojito

Pina Colada

Planters' Punch

Seabreeze

Sex on the Beach

Sidecar

Singapore Sling

Tequila Sunrise

White Russian

Woo Woo

NON-ALCOHOLIC DRINKS

Cinderella

Cola Float

Ginger Pom

Grapefruit Soda

Iced Chocolate Milk

Iced Tea

Lassi (sweet)

Lemon Refresher

Lime and Lemonade

Pink Punch

Raspberry Fizz

Virgin Mary

Virgin Pina Colada

SOME MENU IDEAS

Menu 1 – vegetarian meal for 4

Potato Skins (page 315) and Sour Cream Dip (page 58)

Veggieburgers (page 172)

Oven Chips (page 312)

Salad with Banana Dressing (page 334)

Ice Cream with Chocolate Fudge Sauce (page 373)

Preparation time: 1 hour

Shopping list

8 x 250g potatoes

chives

1 punnet of mustard and cress

1 clove garlic (optional)

packet of mixed lettuce leaves

1 white or red cabbage

1 yellow pepper

1 banana

oil

soy sauce

chilli powder

salt and pepper

jar of chilli relish

white wine vinegar

honey

soft brown sugar

300ml sour cream

butter

4 vegetarian burgers

4 sesame seed burger buns

65g Mars bar

500ml vanilla ice cream

Time plan, to eat at 8:30:

7.30 Measure out the ingredients for the fudge sauce.
Prepare the salad and dressing, but don't add the banana
until you are ready to serve.

7.40 Prepare the potato skins.
Preheat the oven.

7.50 Prepare the oven chips.

8.10 Put the potato skins in the oven.
Prepare the dip.

8.20 Put the oven chips in the oven.

8.30 Turn down the oven temperature.
Put the veggieburgers in the oven and cook as directed on
the packaging.
Serve the potato skins and dip.

8.50 Serve the main course.

Menu 2 – Mexican meal for 4

Crudités (page 52) with Garlic Dip (page 55)

Chicken Fajitas (page 205)

Salad, sour cream, grated cheese

Salsa (page 343)

Guacamole (page 59)

Chocolate Tiramisu (page 364)

Preparation time: 1 hour

Shopping list

4 carrots

2 green peppers

3 red peppers

1 cucumber

1 cauliflower

8 cloves garlic

1 red onion

4 tomatoes

1 small onion

1 lemon

cayenne pepper

2 large ripe avocadoes

salad leaves

450g chicken (about 3 chicken breasts)

soft cream cheese

125ml carton single cream

125ml carton sour cream

100g cheese

250g mascarpone cheese

2 eggs

mayonnaise

oil

chilli powder

ground coriander

230g can chopped tomatoes

tomato purée

8 tortillas

caster sugar

vanilla essence

coffee
miniature brandy

2 chocolate Flakes
box sponge fingers

Time plan, to eat at 8:30:

7.30 Prepare the tiramisu.

7.45 Prepare the salsa.

8.00 Put out the crudités and prepare the dip.

8.00 Prepare the guacamole.

8.05 Prepare the stuffing for fajitas (keep it warm).

8.30 Serve the crudités and dip.

8.50 Serve the main course.

Dîners à Deux These are recipes for those romantic *dîners à deux* to celebrate birthdays, Valentine's Day and other special occasions. You can also prepare them when you are trying to attract that special person into your life. Whether you go to town on the presentation – flowers, candles, etc. – depends on your own style and on how obvious you want your intentions to be!

If you are using wine in the cooking, you could get a measure from the student bar or a can from a supermarket or off-licence. The cans hold two measures (one for the dish, one for the cook!). This saves you having to open a bottle – which you would probably rather drink, or which could be difficult if it is your guest who is bringing the wine.

Menu 1 – Vegetarian for 2

Pasta with Walnuts (page 114)

Side Salad (page 333)

Ricotta with Honey and Pine Nuts (page 361)

Preparation time: 20 minutes

Shopping list

100g mushrooms	50g chopped walnuts
1 little gem lettuce	150g pasta bows or tagliatelle
1 iceberg lettuce	butter
bunch of spring onions	80g Boursin, garlic and herb
bunch of radishes	flavoured
½ cucumber	250g tub ricotta cheese
1 clove garlic	milk
pine nuts	salt and pepper

oil	dried mustard powder
wine vinegar	runny honey

ORDER OF COOKING

1. Prepare the ricotta (do not sprinkle with the nuts).

2. Prepare the salad and dressing.

3. Prepare and cook the pasta.

4. Dress the salad and serve it with the pasta.

5. Sprinkle the ricotta with pine nuts and serve.

Menu 2 – Very special but very easy meal for 2

Prawns in Lime Ginger Butter (page 136)

Lamb in Mustard Cream Sauce (page 143)

Baby Potatoes and Peas (page 309)

Poached Pears in Cider (page 359)

Preparation time: 30 minutes (having cooked the pears in advance)

Shopping list

250g baby new potatoes

80g sugarsnap peas

2 onions

1 clove garlic (optional)

minced ginger

1 lime

2 hard well-shaped pears

1 unwaxed lemon

200g cooked king or tiger prawns

2 lean lamb steaks

double cream

50g butter

80g frozen peas

redcurrant jelly

wholegrain mustard

660ml medium-dry cider

125g caster sugar

1 cinnamon stick

1 vanilla pod (optional)

crusty bread to serve

salt and pepper

Order of cooking

1 Prepare the pears – this can be done well in advance; keep them well covered in the refrigerator.

2 Prepare all the vegetables to the point of cooking.

3 When your guest has arrived, heat and serve the prawns.

4 Put the potatoes in boiling water.

5 After 10 minutes, start cooking the lamb steaks.

6 Start the water boiling for the peas.

7 After turning the lamb steaks, start cooking the peas.

8 Serve the lamb and potatoes and peas. Follow with the pears at your leisure.

COCKTAILS

Appletini

SERVES 1 • PREP 5 min

INGREDIENTS

1 measure (25ml) vodka
1 measure (25ml) apple liqueur
dash of Monin Pomme Verte
    (Green Apple) syrup

METHOD

1 Put all the ingredients in a cocktail shaker with some
   ice.

2 Shake and strain into a martini glass.

B-52

SERVES 1 • PREP 5 min

INGREDIENTS

1 tablespoon Kahlua
1 tablespoon Amaretto
1 tablespoon Baileys Irish Cream

METHOD

1 Layer the Kahlua, amaretto and Irish cream into a shot glass, in that order.

Between-the-sheets

SERVES 1 • PREP 5 min

INGREDIENTS

1 *tablespoon brandy*
1 *tablespoon light rum*
1 *tablespoon triple sec or*
   Cointreau
1 *teaspoon lemon juice*

METHOD

1 Put all the ingredients in a cocktail shaker with some ice.

2 Shake and strain into a shot glass.

Black Russian

SERVES 1 • PREP 5 min

INGREDIENTS

2 measures (50ml) vodka
1 measure (25ml) Kahlua
 or Tia Maria
cola

METHOD

1 Put the vodka and Kahlua in a cocktail shaker with some ice.

2 Shake and pour into a long glass.

3 Top up with cola.

Brandy Alexander

SERVES 1 • PREP 5 min

INGREDIENTS

1 *measure (25ml) brandy*
1 *measure (25ml) Kahlua*
1 *measure (25ml) cream*

METHOD

1 Put all the ingredients in a cocktail shaker with some ice.

2 Shake and strain into a cocktail glass.

Caipirinha

SERVES 1 • PREP 5 min

INGREDIENTS

1 *lime*
1 *tablespoon soft brown sugar*
2 *measures (50ml) cachaça*

METHOD

1 Quarter the lime lengthwise, then cut each quarter in half crosswise and put the pieces in a tumbler.

2 Add the sugar to the glass, then muddle the lime pieces by pounding and pressing with a wooden spoon until the sugar is dissolved into the lime juice.

3 Fill the glass with ice and add the cachaça. Stir well.

Cosmopolitan

SERVES 1 • PREP 5 min

INGREDIENTS

2 measures (50ml) vodka

*1 measure (250ml) triple sec
or Cointreau*

1 measure (25ml) cranberry juice

½ measure (12.5ml) lime juice

METHOD

1 Put all the ingredients in a cocktail shaker with some
ice.

2 Shake and strain into a cocktail glass.

FBI

You do need a blender for this one. Ice cream does open up a whole host of new recipes for cocktails – I'm thinking of using this recipe with various Ben & Jerry ice creams instead of the creamy vanilla ice cream here. Just think of all the concoctions you could come up with . . .

SERVES 1 • PREP 5 min

INGREDIENTS

1 *measure (25ml) Baileys Irish Cream*
1 *measure (25ml) Kahlua*
½ *measure (12.5ml) vodka*
2 *tablespoons vanilla ice cream*

METHOD

1 Blend all the ingredients with a few crushed ice cubes.

2 Pour into a tumbler.

TIP If you have a strong enough blender, you can crush the ice cubes in it. If not, put the ice cubes into a clean tea towel, twist securely and bash it thoroughly.

Harvey Wallbanger

SERVES 1 • PREP 5 min

INGREDIENTS

1 measure (25ml) vodka
orange juice
1 measure (25ml) Galliano

METHOD

1 Put ice into a long straight glass.

2 Add vodka and top up with orange juice. Stir.

3 Add the Galliano slowly, so that most of it floats on top.

FREDDY FUDPUCKER

Substitute tequila for the vodka.

Head Honcho

SERVES 1 • PREP 5 min

INGREDIENTS

1 measure (25ml) tequila
1 measure (25ml) Kahlua
1 teaspoon lime juice

METHOD

1 Put all the ingredients in a cocktail shaker with some ice.

2 Shake and strain into a martini glass.

June Bug

SERVES 1 • PREP 5 min

INGREDIENTS

1 *measure (25ml) Malibu*
½ measure (12.5ml) Midori
½ measure (12.5ml) crème de bananes
dash of lime

METHOD

1 Put all the ingredients in a cocktail shaker with some ice.

2 Shake and strain into a martini glass.

Kamikaze

SERVES 1 • PREP 5 min

INGREDIENTS

1 tablespoon vodka
1 tablespoon triple sec
   or Cointreau
1 tablespoon lime juice

METHOD

1 Put all the ingredients in a cocktail shaker with some ice.

2 Shake and strain into a shot glass.

Long Island Iced Tea

Do note that this recipe serves 2.

SERVES 2 • PREP 5 min

INGREDIENTS

1 *measure (25ml) vodka*
1 *measure (25ml) gin*
1 *measure (25ml) light rum*
1 *measure (25ml) tequila*
1 *measure (25ml) triple sec or*
   Cointreau
1 *measure (25ml) lemon*
   or lime juice
2 *teaspoons sugar syrup*
   or caster sugar
cola

METHOD

1 Put all the ingredients in a cocktail shaker with some ice.

2 Put some ice in 2 long straight glasses (or a teapot).

3 Shake the cocktail shaker and strain the cocktail into glasses or the teapot.

4 Top up with cola. If you are using a teapot, pour the drink into teacups.

Lynchburg Lemonade

SERVES 1 • PREP 5 min

INGREDIENTS

2 measures (50ml) Jack Daniels whiskey
1 measure (25ml) lemon juice
½ measure (12.5ml) sugar syrup
lemonade

METHOD

1 Put ice into a long straight glass.

2 Pour in the whiskey, lemon juice and sugar syrup. Stir.

3 Top up with lemonade.

Mai Tai

SERVES 1 • PREP 5 min

INGREDIENTS

1 measure (25ml) light rum
1 measure (25ml) dark rum
1 measure (25ml) tequila
1 measure (25ml) triple sec
  or Cointreau
orange juice
dash of grenadine

METHOD

1 Put some ice in a tall straight glass, add the rums, tequila and triple sec or Cointreau.

2 Top up with orange juice.

3 Add a dash of grenadine and stir well.

Margarita

SERVES 1 • PREP 5 min

INGREDIENTS

2 measures (50ml) tequila

2 measures (50ml) triple sec
or Cointreau

1 measure (25ml) lime juice

METHOD

1 Put all the ingredients in a cocktail shaker with some ice.

2 Shake and strain into a margarita cocktail glass.

TIP This is traditionally served in a salt-rimmed glass. You will need two plates for this: the first filled with lime juice, the second with salt. Dip the glass rim in the lime juice and then the salt.

Martini

SERVES 1 • PREP 5 min

INGREDIENTS

3 measures (75ml) gin
1 measure (25ml) dry vermouth

METHOD

1 Put the ingredients in a cocktail shaker with some ice.

2 Shake and strain into a martini glass.

Melon Daiquiri

SERVES 1 • PREP 5 min

INGREDIENTS

2 measures (50ml) white rum
2 measures (50ml) Midori
1 measure (25ml) lime juice

METHOD

1 Put the ingredients in a cocktail shaker with some ice.

2 Shake and strain into a margarita glass.

TIP Many different flavoured daiquiris can be made using this basic recipe but substituting different liqueurs for the Midori. Any fruit-flavoured liqueurs work well. If you have a blender, you can also use fresh fruit or even fruit-flavoured ice cream to produce frozen daiquiris.

COCONUT DAIQUIRI

Use Malibu instead of the Midori.

Mojito

SERVES 1 • PREP 5 min

INGREDIENTS

1 lime
20 fresh mint leaves
2 teaspoons caster sugar
2 measures (50ml) white rum
soda water

METHOD

1   Quarter the lime lengthwise, then cut each quarter in half crosswise and put the pieces in a tumbler.

2   Add the mint and sugar to the glass, then muddle the lime pieces by pounding and pressing with a wooden spoon until the sugar is dissolved into the lime juice.

3   Add some ice and pour over the rum.

4   Add soda water to taste and stir well.

Pina Colada

SERVES 1 • PREP 5 min

INGREDIENTS

2 measures (50ml) light rum
2 measures (50ml) coconut cream
pineapple juice

METHOD

1 Put the rum and coconut cream in a cocktail shaker with some ice.

2 Shake well and strain into a large cocktail glass.

3 Top up with pineapple juice and stir well before serving.

TIP If you have a blender, this is very nice when blended.

Planters' Punch

SERVES 1 • PREP 5 min

INGREDIENTS

2 measures (50ml) dark rum

2 measures (50ml) orange juice

1 tablespoon lime juice

1 tablespoon sugar syrup
   or 1 teaspoon caster sugar

dash of Angostura Bitters

METHOD

1 Put all the ingredients except the bitters in a cocktail shaker with some ice.

2 Shake and then strain into a tumbler.

3 Add a dash of bitters and stir before serving.

TIP This was originally made with orgeat syrup, which can be quite difficult to find. If you can get it, substitute 1 measure (25ml) orgeat syrup for the sugar syrup and Angostura Bitters.

Seabreeze

SERVES 1 • PREP 5 min

INGREDIENTS

2 measures (50ml) vodka
3 measures (75ml) cranberry juice
3 measures (75ml) grapefruit juice

METHOD

1 Put some ice in a tall straight glass and add all the ingredients.

2 Stir well and serve.

Sex on the Beach

SERVES 1 • PREP 5 min

INGREDIENTS

1 measure (25ml) vodka
1 measure (25ml) peach schnapps
1 tablespoon orange juice
1 tablespoon cranberry juice
1 tablespoon lemon juice

METHOD

1 Put all the ingredients in a cocktail shaker with some ice.

2 Shake and strain into a tumbler.

TIP   I went to Sussex University, situated on the outskirts of Brighton, which has a shingle beach. Therefore, this was often served with ice 'on the rocks' or sex on the beach Brighton style! There are so many different flavoured vodkas and schnapps now that you can use this basic recipe to make any number of concoctions that you can then name yourself . . .

Sidecar

SERVES 1 • PREP 5 min

INGREDIENTS

1 *measure (25ml) brandy*
1 *tablespoon triple sec*
   or Cointreau
1 *tablespoon lemon juice*

METHOD

1 Put all the ingredients in a cocktail shaker with some ice.

2 Shake and then strain into a martini glass.

TIP I have known people make this with equal measures of brandy, triple sec and lemon juice (it's quicker and easier to make this way) – it's all a matter of taste.

Singapore Sling

SERVES 1 • PREP 5 min

INGREDIENTS

2 measures (50ml) gin
1 measure (25ml) cherry brandy
½ measure (12.5ml) triple sec
  or Cointreau
1 measure (25ml) lime juice
1 teaspoon sugar syrup
  or caster sugar
soda water

METHOD

1 Put all the ingredients except the soda water in a cocktail shaker with some ice.

2 Shake and strain into a tall straight glass.

3 Top up with soda water.

4 Stir and serve.

Tequila Sunrise

SERVES 1 • PREP 5 min

INGREDIENTS

1 measure (25ml) tequila
orange juice
1 teaspoon grenadine

METHOD

1   Put ice into a long straight glass.

2   Add the tequila and fill up the glass with orange juice. Stir.

3   Add the grenadine – do not stir. Serve.

White Russian

SERVES 1 • PREP 5 min

INGREDIENTS

1 *measure (25ml) vodka*
1 *measure (25ml) Kahlua*
1 *measure (25ml) cream*

METHOD

1 Put all the ingredients in a cocktail shaker with some ice.

2 Shake and strain into a martini glass.

Woo Woo

SERVES 1 • PREP 5 min

INGREDIENTS

1 measure (25ml) vodka
1 measure (25ml) peach schnapps
2 measures (50ml) cranberry juice

METHOD

1 Put all the ingredients in a cocktail shaker with some ice.

2 Shake and strain into a martini glass.

TIP The woo woo is a variation of sex on the beach. It can also be made with just a half measure of cranberry juice or made into a long drink and topped up with cranberry juice. The peach schnapps can also be changed. I've had a very nice one made with Malibu – aptly named a Malibu woo woo!

NON-ALCOHOLIC DRINKS

Cinderella

SERVES 1 • PREP 5 min

INGREDIENTS

2 measures (50ml) orange juice
2 measures (50ml) pineapple juice
1 measure (25ml) lemon juice
1 teaspoon sugar syrup

METHOD

1 Put all the ingredients in a cocktail shaker with some ice.

2 Shake and strain into a cocktail glass.

Cola Float

SERVES 1 • PREP 5 min

INGREDIENTS

cola
vanilla ice cream

METHOD

1 Fill your chosen glass ⅔ full with cola.

2 Take a large scoop of ice cream and place it in the glass.

TIP   This is best served with a straw and a spoon.

Ginger Pom

SERVES 1 • PREP 5 min

INGREDIENTS

150ml pomegranate juice
100ml ginger ale

METHOD

1 Put ice in a tall straight glass.

2 Add the ingredients and stir.

Grapefruit Soda

SERVES 1 • PREP 5 min

INGREDIENTS

150ml *grapefruit juice*
100ml *soda water*

METHOD

1 Put ice in a tall straight glass.

2 Add the ingredients and stir.

Iced Chocolate Milk

SERVES 1 • PREP 5 min

INGREDIENTS

150ml chocolate-flavoured milk

METHOD

1 Put the chocolate milk in a cocktail shaker with some ice.

2 Shake and strain into a cocktail glass.

TIP   You can also buy banana- and strawberry-flavoured milk. These make great mocktails.

Iced Tea

SERVES 6 • PREP 10 min + STANDING TIME

INGREDIENTS

6 English Breakfast teabags
3 tablespoons caster sugar
1.5 litres boiling water
12 sprigs of fresh mint
250ml fresh orange juice
juice of ½ lime
juice of ½ lemon
1 orange, sliced

METHOD

1 Make up the tea with the teabags, sugar, boiling water and half of the mint.

2 Let it stand for 20 minutes and then remove the teabags and the mint.

3 Leave until completely cold and then add the orange juice, the juices from the lime and lemon and the orange slices with the rest of the mint.

4 Add ice just before serving.

Lassi (sweet)

SERVES 2 • PREP 5 min

INGREDIENTS

150ml natural yogurt
300ml water
2 tablespoons caster sugar

METHOD

1 Mix all the ingredients together.

2 Serve in tumblers, preferably over ice.

TIP You can make a sour version by omitting the sugar and adding
1 tablespoon of lemon juice and a pinch of salt.

Lemon Refresher

SERVES 1 • PREP 5 min

INGREDIENTS

200ml fresh lemonade
50ml apple juice

METHOD

1 Put ice in a tall straight glass.

2 Add the ingredients and stir.

Lime and Lemonade

SERVES 1 • PREP 5 min

INGREDIENTS

1 measure (25ml) lime cordial
lemonade

METHOD

1 Put some ice in a long straight glass.

2 Pour in the lime cordial and top up with lemonade.

Pink Punch

SERVES 6 • PREP 5 min

INGREDIENTS

500ml cranberry juice
500ml sparkling apple juice
500ml fresh orange juice
1 orange, sliced

METHOD

1 Chill all the ingredients before using.

2 Just before you are ready to serve, mix all the ingredients together in a jug or large bowl. Use plenty of ice.

Raspberry Fizz

SERVES 1 • PREP 5 min

INGREDIENTS

100ml apple and raspberry juice
150ml Appletiser

METHOD

1 Put ice in a tall straight glass.

2 Add the ingredients and stir.

Virgin Mary

SERVES 1 • PREP 5 min

INGREDIENTS

250ml tomato juice
dash of Worcestershire sauce
pinch of celery salt

METHOD

1 Put some ice in a tall straight glass.

2 Pour in the tomato juice and add the Worcestershire sauce. Stir.

3 Add the celery salt. Serve.

Virgin Pina Colada

SERVES 1 • PREP 5 min

INGREDIENTS

100ml coconut milk or
  cream of coconut (Coco Lopez)
100ml pineapple juice

METHOD

1 Put the ingredients in a cocktail shaker with some ice.

2 Put some ice in a tall, straight glass.

3 Shake and strain into the glass.

TIP   This is even better if made in a blender, so that it's really frothy.

IDEAS ON HOW TO USE LEFTOVER INGREDIENTS

CRÈME FRAÎCHE

Spaghetti Tricolor (page 111)

Fruity Curry Sauce (page 340)

Mushroom Stroganoff (page 87)

Avocado and Salsa Tortillas (page 60)

EGGS

Chinese Rice with Omelette (page 126)

Cheese and Tomato Omelette (page 29)

Egg and Lentil Curry (page 137)

Huevos Rancheros (page 26)

Cheese Omelette (page 27)

Frittata (page 32)

Pasta Frittata (page 117)

Pipérade (page 89)

Scrambled Curried Eggs with Chapattis (page 20)

Tomato and Spring Onion Omelette (page 28)

HERBS

Roasted New Potatoes (page 319)

Tomato and Spring Onion Omelette (page 28)

Tzatziki (page 54)

Tabbouleh (page 335)

Tuscan Bean Soup (page 154)

KORMA CURRY PASTE

Fruity Curry Sauce (page 340)

Vegetable Biryani (page 192)

Vegetable Korma (page 235)

OYSTER SAUCE

Stir-fried Beef in Oyster Sauce (page 122)

Chilli Vegetables and Noodles (page 123)

Chinese Vegetables and Noodles (page 129)

SEMOLINA

Roast Potatoes (page 317)

Roman Gnocchi (page 249)

SOFT CHEESE

Dolcelatte-dressed Spaghetti and Leeks (page 103)

Tuna-stuffed Jacket Potatoes (page 83)

Soft cheese mixed with grated or chopped celery or chopped spring onions makes a good filling for sandwiches or rolls.

SOFT CHEESE WITH GARLIC

Creamed Leek and Courgette Sauce (page 115)

Broccoli Sauce (page 115)

Pasta with Cheese 'n' Garlic Sauce (page 120)

Jacket Potatoes Filled with Garlic Cheese and Mushrooms (page 82)

Creamy Courgettes and Walnuts (page 88)

SOUR CREAM

Avocado and Salsa Tortillas (page 60)

Tandoori Chicken (page 257)

Sour cream and cheese can be used as a topping for baked potatoes.

SUN-DRIED TOMATOES

Spaghetti Tricolor (page 111)

Vegetarian Pasta Bake (page 233)

Sun-dried Tomato Risotto (page 99)

THAI RED CURRY PASTE

Thai Prawns (page 121)

Thai Prawn Curry (page 187)

Thai red curry paste can be fried with onions and then added to coconut milk to make a base for a hot and spicy soup.

VEG

½ GREEN PEPPER

Chicken and Banana Creole (page 197)

Special Fried Rice (page 66)

Chilli con Carne (page 203)

Spicy Rice (page 140)

½ RED PEPPER

Cheesy Rice (page 91)

Sweet 'n' Sour Vegetables (page 132)

½ SMALL ONION

Melted Cheese and Tuna Bagel (page 44)

Spicy Rice (page 140)

Sliced thinly can also be used in toasted sandwiches.

SPRING ONIONS

Tomato and Spring Onion Omelette (page 28)

Avocado and Salsa Tortillas (page 60)

Chicken Chow Mein (page 133)

Spaghetti Tunagnese (page 116)

Thai Lamb (page 124)

Thai Noodles (page 131)

Index

Note: Due to their ubiquity, vegetarian dishes are not listed separately, but are indicated by a bracketed 'v'.